Understanding criminology
Current theoretical debates

CRIME AND JUSTICE
Series editor: Mike Maguire
University College of Wales, College of Cardiff

Crime and Justice is a series of short introductory texts on central topics in criminology. The books in this series are written for students by internationally renowned authors. Each book tackles a key area within criminology, providing a concise and up-to-date overview of the principal concepts, theories, methods and findings relating to the area. Taken as a whole, the *Crime and Justice* series will cover all the core components of an undergraduate criminology course.

Published titles

Understanding youth and crime
Sheila Brown

Understanding crime data
Clive Coleman and Jenny Moynihan

Understanding justice
Barbara A. Hudson

Understanding crime prevention
Gordon Hughes

Understanding criminology
Sandra Walklate

Understanding criminology
Current theoretical debates

Sandra Walklate

Open University Press
Buckingham · Philadelphia

Open University Press
Celtic Court
22 Ballmoor
Buckingham
MK18 1XW

email: enquiries@openup.co.uk
world wide web: http://www.openup.co.uk

and
325 Chestnut Street
Philadelphia, PA 19106, USA

First Published 1998
Reprinted 1998, 1999

A catalogue record of this book is available from the British Library

ISBN 0 335 19362 5 (hb)   0 335 19361 7 (pb)

Library of Congress Cataloging-in-Publication Data
Walklate, Sandra.
    Understanding criminology: current theoretical debates/Sandra Walklate.
        p.   cm.
    Includes bibliographical references and index.
    ISBN 0-335-19362-5. – ISBN 0-335-19361-7 (pbk.)
    1. Criminology.   2. Criminal anthropology.
    HV6025.W356   1997
    364–dc21   97-15404
                                                                    CIP

Typeset by Type Study, Scarborough
Printed in Great Britain by Biddles Ltd, Guildford and King's Lynn

Contents

Series editor's foreword

This is the third in a series of textbooks on important areas of debate within the fields of criminology, criminal justice and penology. The broad aim of the series is to provide relatively short and accessible texts, written by experienced lecturers and researchers, which will give undergraduates or postgraduates a solid grounding in the relevant area and, it is hoped, a taste for the subject which will lead them to explore the literature further. Although aimed primarily at students new to the field, and although written as far as possible in plain language, the books do not give the false impression that they are dealing with a simple subject, easily mastered. On the contrary, all the authors aim to 'stretch' readers and to encourage them to approach criminological knowledge and theory in a critical and questioning frame of mind.

Sandra Walklate's book provides a valuable introduction to current debates in criminological theory. Many student textbooks provide a standard chronological account of the history of criminological thought, starting with Lombroso and the rise of positivism, dwelling at length on the sociologists who dominated the discipline in the United States from the 1930s to the 1960s, and perhaps finishing with a brief chapter or two on deviancy theory, radical criminology and/or left realism. However, few have adopted Sandra Walklate's refreshing approach of taking as their central focus some of the key concerns which have dominated both theory and research since the mid-1970s. While giving due deference to the early pioneers, she shows that criminology is now a very different (and far more complex) discipline, in which theorists have to take account of many new kinds of data, major changes in social structures and institutions, and developments in other academic fields. The core issues she grapples with include the relationships between crime and gender, crime and poverty, crime and the family and – fundamental to understanding current discourses about crime – the changing relationship between the citizen and the state. In exploring such questions she provides clear expositions of the contributions, strengths and weaknesses of, *inter alia*, feminist theory, left realism and right realism, victimology, and postmodernist approaches to criminology, as well as of theories built around the controversial concept of the 'underclass'.

The first two books in the Crime and Justice series covered penal theory (Barbara A. Hudson) and crime data and statistics (Clive Coleman and Jenny Moynihan). Others in the pipeline include youth crime and justice (Sheila Brown and John Macmillan), sentencing and the penal system (Mike Maguire), crime prevention (Gordon Hughes) and crime and social exclusion (Loraine Gelsthorpe). All are central topics in the growing field of crime-related studies in universities, and each book makes an ideal foundation text for core courses or modules. As an aid to understanding, clear summaries are provided at regular intervals, and a glossary of key terms and concepts is a feature of every book. In addition, to help students expand their knowledge in specific areas, recommendations for further reading are given at the end of each chapter.

Finally, I must again record my gratitude to Roy Light and John Skelton for the original suggestion that I become involved in editing a series of this nature, as well as to Jacinta Evans, Nick Evans, Justin Vaughan, Joan Malherbe, Pat Lee and Gaynor Clements (past and present staff of Open University Press) for their help in bringing it to fruition. Most of all, I thank the authors, who have all made my job as series editor both simple and pleasurable.

Mike Maguire
University of Wales, Cardiff

Preface and acknowledgements

As so many people now recognize in higher education, the changing context of the teaching, learning and research environments sometimes means that deadlines are not always met. This book has had a particularly long gestation period and that has not only been as a result of a changing work context. Events in one's personal life also take their toll. It is for this reason that I am especially grateful to Mike Maguire, the series editor, and Justin Vaughan, at Open University Press, for hanging on in there with me. Their patience was deeply valued. Thanks are also due to my colleagues in the Department of Criminology at the University of Keele for allowing me to get on with things in my own way. Especially important has been the support of both Lynn Hancock and Rachel McKittrick. No matter what they thought of where I was heading, they stuck with me when it mattered most. Last, but by no means least, credit is also due to my keenest critic and my keenest supporter, my partner Ron Wardale. His real life experience and intellectual vision are always respected and appreciated.

chapter one

Introduction: understanding some key features of criminology

A book, like this one, entitled *Understanding Criminology*, begs a number of important questions about its subject matter in the very title assigned to it. Such a title makes a number of claims: that there is an area of study clearly identifiable as criminology, that that area of study has a clearly definable subject matter, that there is some agreement as to what that subject matter comprises, and that there is a range of concepts which are commonly used and commonly understood with which to talk about that subject matter. Each of these claims is contentious. In this Introduction we shall endeavour to examine the nature of these claims in an effort to appreciate the problems inherent in talking about crime. First of all, it will be useful to develop some appreciation of what characterizes criminology as a discipline and how its subject matter might be defined.

Some domain assumptions within criminology as a discipline

Criminology as a discipline has been described as a rather tenuous area of study (Rock, 1986). In other words, it is an area of study not defined by a particular unit of social reality (as psychology is definitively concerned with the individual, or sociology with social relationships), it is defined by its substantive concern: crime. Consequently, it is a discipline inhabited by practitioners, policy makers and academics, all of whom share a common interest in that substantive issue but all of whom may be committed to quite different disciplinary ways of thinking about it, from psychiatry to sociology. This, then, gives criminology a multidisciplinary rather than a unidisciplinary character.

Additionally it is important to note that criminology, like any other area of inquiry, has made efforts to create for itself an intellectual history despite its multidisciplinary character. That intellectual history has been marked on many occasions by a process of articulating a sense of continuity between the concerns of what might be called the early criminological thought of the sixteenth and seventeenth centuries (what Rock, 1994, calls shadow criminology or ur-criminology) and the later concerns of the eighteenth and nineteenth centuries. Whether or not such a continuity exists is a moot point.

As Garland (1994) says, it is possible to identify a variety of ways, historically, in which talk about crime entered public discourse, through the work of essayists and clergymen, for example. However, to argue that there was some continuous thread of common concern between these different ways of talking about crime glosses not only the differences between them but also the historically contingent and specific nature of some of those concerns. This does not mean that views about crime (roguery, sinfulness, or other ways of depicting offensive behaviour) were not being articulated or did not represent authentic concerns. It does mean, however, that it may be misplaced to talk of those concerns as if they represented some coherent body of evolving knowledge called criminology. Indeed, Garland (1988: 1) states that, ' "Criminology" as a professional academic discipline did not exist in Britain before 1935, and was established only gradually and precariously thereafter.'

The question remains, however, of what constitutes the backcloth against which the discipline of criminology emerged: what characterized that emergent discipline and influenced its later development? Despite the presence of different ways of talking about crime or criminal behaviour, there is a common thread to the construction of 'criminological' knowledge about such behaviour. That common thread can be traced historically through the influence of the Enlightenment the common adherence to one way of thinking about knowledge and the knowledge construction process – positivism. It will be of some value to consider the influence of these ideas in a little more detail.

Criminology and the Enlightenment

Criminology, like other social science disciplines, is often characterized as being rooted in 'modern' ideas. What is meant by the term 'modern' is, however, open to interpretation. In this context modern refers to the features of social and cultural life which, arguably, became embedded in social structural processes consequent to the impact of the Enlightenment. The form of that impact can be characterized in a number of different ways.

Cooke (1990) suggests that the Enlightenment had the effect of producing the belief that

> Reason could be used to make the future a malleable one, and could interrupt the flow of history, overturn traditional hegemonies. Modernity was now to be understood as the very expression of individual and collective reason to bring about the achievement of some great social project.
>
> (Cooke, 1990: 5)

This belief in the power of reason, and of the reasoning capacities of men in particular (Seidler, 1994), had a powerful effect on the role that other beliefs had previously had in society, especially religious beliefs. Indeed the belief in the power of reason, in some respects, not only took the place of religion but also put in its place a belief in the reasonable power of science and the scientific enterprise. This requires further explanation.

In our current everyday lives we are surrounded by technology and technological developments which reflect features of a modern society which have come to be taken for granted – computers, cars, televisions, etc. Science and technology have been remarkably successful in changing the nature of people's everyday lives in quite fundamental ways in the production of such artefacts. However, the belief in the role and importance of science in modern societies is, arguably, more fundamental than even the production of such artefacts suggests.

Underpinning this kind of productive process lies a presumption that it is through the knowledge produced by science that humans could control the environment (nature). This presumption not only became rooted in the natural sciences, but also became rooted in the emergent social sciences. In other words, the social sciences, modelled on the natural sciences, could provide the data on which social life, including social problems, could be not just managed but also controlled. These beliefs, embedded in the notion of a modern society, have underpinned criminological work since its inception and have tied criminology implicitly to the policy-making process: that is to the belief that policies could be formulated to better control and/or manage criminal behaviour. The basis on which those policies were (are) to be formulated is connected with the influence of positivism, mentioned above, and how the knowledge production process is to be understood.

Many reviews of the origins of criminology refer to the influence of positivism. Positivism is a term used to describe one way of thinking about the basis on which knowledge can claim to be scientific. The claim to produce scientific knowledge has been made by criminology through its historical commitment to objectivity; understanding the determined nature of criminal behaviour; and by its ability to measure criminal behaviour (Taylor *et al.*, 1973). These ideas, that criminal behaviour can be objectively measured through understanding the social, psychological or biological factors which produce it, reflect a commitment to a view of the scientific endeavour as fundamentally being concerned to produce universal explanations.

This desire to construct an explanation of crime which would apply to all situations has constituted a key characteristic of criminology and is connected to the implicit desire to formulate policy. Of course, the kinds of explanations which have been produced have varied according to the disciplinary concerns of the producers. This, in part, accounts for the confusion which academic criminology both reflects and thrives on. It also, in part, contributes to the tensions between academic talk about crime and common sense talk about crime.

As an area of study, then, peopled in this way, and informed by (historically at least) a fundamental concern to produce universal explanations of crime, contributes to some of the confusion as to whether or not there is anything clearly definable as *criminological* knowledge. Moreover, these factors also make it especially important to understand what is being said, by whom, and how that knowledge has been generated. In other words, there are not only competing theoretical perspectives on crime (as there are competing perspectives in other social science areas of study) but also quite distinct competing presumptions about the unit of analysis with which to even begin to think about the crime problem; from individual biology through to the role of the state.

To summarize: in the preface to his book *Talking about Crime and Criminals* Gibbons (1994) has this to say:

> The title of this book speaks of 'talking about crime' and is intended to draw attention to the fact that much of the time criminologists literally don't know quite what they are talking about. Much of what passes for theorising in criminology involves fuzzy or undefined concepts, propositions that are implicit rather than explicit and/or that are internally inconsistent, and kindred other problems of exposition or logical structure.
>
> (Gibbons, 1994: ix)

Of course, criminologists are not the only ones to suffer from problems such as these. Lack of clarity and fuzziness are problems inherent in both professional and 'common-sense' discourses on crime. Some of these difficulties lie in both understanding the nature of criminology as a discipline as well as understanding what influences how definitions of criminal behaviour are constructed and how talk about crime is constructed. These are separate though interconnected issues worthy of further exploration.

How to define the criminal?

Defining that behaviour which counts as criminal behaviour and that behaviour which does not is neither an easy nor a straightforward process. It is clear, of course, that what is or is not permitted by the criminal law can be taken as the point of reference which defines the kind of behaviour with which criminologists are concerned. In this sense it is possible to say that the substantial concern of criminology is lawbreaking behaviour rather than criminal behaviour. This clearly differentiates the kind of behaviour with which criminology might be concerned from the more emotive use of the term 'criminal' itself, the use of which potentially can prejudge the guilt of the offender or can draw on more deeply embedded notions of 'wickedness'. Both of these tendencies not only fuel debates on crime but also can serve to contribute to the fuzziness associated with those debates.

Taking the law as the point at which behaviour comes under the scrutiny of criminology certainly offers up for analysis a very broad and wide ranging set of concerns. Moreover, the implications of defining criminological concerns in this way need to be spelt out a little more clearly.

First, such a definition places the law at the centre of defining behaviour as criminal or otherwise rather than placing the behaviour itself at the centre of criminological concerns. In so doing, however, it must be remembered that such a reference point can always and only define behaviour in this way at any one particular historical moment. Laws change. Some behaviours are newly defined as criminal (lawbreaking) others are de-criminalized (defined as non-lawbreaking). The age of homosexual consent constitutes a good example of an area of the law in which changes have taken place over a relatively short historical period of time. The presumption of this book will be, however, that the central concern of criminology is lawbreaking behaviour.

Second, defining criminological concerns in this way inevitably directs any talk of understanding criminal behaviour towards, in part, understanding the processes whereby that behaviour has come to be defined as criminal that is understanding how and why laws change. An emphasis of this kind is somewhat different from an emphasis that focuses on the inherent characteristics of individuals as predefining their criminality. Characteristics which, it has been argued, predispose some individuals to engage in criminal activities, like, for example, having a particular kind of personality or possessing a certain chromosomal pattern (see Chapter 2 for a thematic development of this kind of approach). So, defining the central concern of criminology as being lawbreaking behaviour implies that those concerns are much more centrally focused on the *social processes* which lead to some behaviours but not others as being defined as criminal and therefore being subjected to 'crime talk'.

Indeed, there exists a good deal of common-sense knowledge about crime and criminal victimization (some would say overdramatized knowledge as a result of the influence of the media, see pp. 6–10), this knowledge, for some of the reasons suggested above, often sits uncomfortably with the rather more tenuous and circumscribed knowledge produced within a discipline called criminology which frequently does not agree with itself. These issues notwithstanding there is, however, some agreement on some fairly general criminological 'truths', which frequently challenge the rather more dramatic media images of crime with which we may be more familiar.

Therefore having, it is hoped, clarified one way of defining the kind of behaviour with which criminology might be concerned, it will be useful to explore some common perceptions about what criminal behaviour is like, who is likely to engage in it, and what influences those perceptions.

What influences talk about crime?

Felson (1994) points to a number of fallacies that people often share about crime. One of these fallacies he refers to as the 'dramatic fallacy'. By this he means the extent to which media portrayals of crime, both factual and fictional, serve to equip individuals with particular images of the nature of crime, criminals, and criminal victimization. These images tend to overplay the extraordinary crime and underplay the ordinary, routine, mundane nature of most criminal offences which take place.

The dramatization of crime in this way, however, informs common sense talk about crime. Moreover such dramatizations not only inform common sense talk, but also frequently inform political talk. Such talk, given its dramatic influences, is often emotive in form and content and constitutes the backcloth against which criminological talk can look vague and fuzzy indeed. However, the power and influence of such images make the case all the stronger for clarity from criminology and criminologists. That such clarity appears to be absent is in part attributable to the nature of the discipline as well as to the nature of its chosen subject matter as discussed above.

However, Felson (1994) goes on to argue that media images of crime often serve to fuel a number of other fallacies about criminal behaviour. In particular they fuel what he calls the 'age fallacy' and the 'ingenuity fallacy'. In other words, media images leave us with the impression that both victims and offenders are rather more middle aged than they actually are, and in addition, give the impression that in order to commit crime it is necessary to be daring and ingenious. Media portrayals also frequently distort the nature of the role of the criminal justice professionals in the crime business and what they are more or less capable of. None of these images is borne out by the empirical data on crime but they nevertheless infuse commonly held images of crime. Such a statement then begs the question of what it is that is known about crime (lawbreaking behaviour)? What, then, might a criminological 'truth' comprise?

What do we know about crime?

In answering a question such as this it is usual to refer to the various sources of statistical information on crime. These sources of information include official statistics, survey statistics (especially criminal victimization survey data) and self-report studies. Each of these sources of information offers different kinds of information about crime (and criminal victimization). Their respective strengths and weaknesses are discussed by Coleman and Moynihan (1996). Suffice it to say that on the basis of information of this kind and a whole range of different academic studies of crime Braithwaite (1989) has identified a number of criminological 'truths'.

Braithwaite (1989: 44–9) states that there are thirteen 'facts' about crime which criminology needs to explain and which more common sense knowledge can sometimes fail to appreciate:

1 Crime is committed disproportionately by males.
2 Crime is perpetrated disproportionately by 15–25-year-olds.
3 Crime is committed disproportionately by unmarried people.
4 Crime is committed disproportionately by people living in large cities.
5 Crime is committed disproportionately by people who have experienced high residential mobility and who live in areas characterized by high residential mobility.
6 Young people who are strongly attached to their school are less likely to engage in crime.
7 Young people who have high educational and occupational aspirations are less likely to engage in crime.
8 Young people who do poorly at school are more likely to engage in crime.
9 Young people who are strongly attached to their parents are less likely to engage in crime.
10 Young people who have friendships with criminals are more likely to engage in crime themselves.
11 People who believe strongly in complying with the law are less likely to violate the law.
12 For both men and women, being at the bottom of the class structure, whether measured by socio-economic status, socio-economic status of the area in which the person lives, being unemployed, being a member of an oppressed racial minority, increases rates of offending for all types of crime apart from those for which opportunities are systematically less available to the poor.
13 Crime rates have been increasing since the Second World War in most countries, developed and developing. The only case of a country which has been clearly shown to have had a falling crime rate in this period is Japan.

These facts which a theory of crime 'ought to fit' can be tempered in a number of ways. In some respects, for example, they do not quite resonate with the phenomenon of 'white collar crime'. That kind of lawbreaking behaviour appears to be committed by older, married males. Moreover, caution does need to be asserted more generally about these 'facts' given that they are (and can only be) derived from the variety of sources of information available about lawbreaking behaviour – sources of information which are always going to be incomplete in some way or another. Such caveats notwithstanding, such 'facts' certainly challenge some aspects of common-sense knowledge about crime and criminal behaviour.

For example, common-sense knowledge about crime, for the most part, renders implicit that most crime is committed by men. Indeed, this criminological 'fact' has until the mid-1980s also remained implicit in much criminological talk about crime (see Chapter 5). Common-sense knowledge about crime (and again up until the mid-1980s, much criminological knowledge) also renders invisible the hidden nature of much criminal activity; for example, 'domestic' violence, rape in marriage, buying stolen goods, failure to enforce Health and Safety Regulations in the workplace, fraudulent activities from business corporations. Indeed, in many respects much criminological work has focused on that kind of lawbreaking behaviour which common-sense understandings of crime would most readily identify – juvenile delinquency, burglary and street crime.

However, identifying such 'facts', as Braithwaite (1989) does, contentious though some aspects of them might be, does not necessarily provide us with an explanation of them. So, while much criminological work has been concerned to measure the nature and extent of crime, that is, there has been a keen empirical focus central to the discipline, in order to make sense of those 'facts', it is necessary to try to explain them. What might such an explanation consist of? Braithwaite's list of 'facts' foregrounds social characteristics: general patterns of variables characteristic of social groups or social processes which have been identified by more than one empirical study as contributing to the propensity to engage in lawbreaking behaviour. Such social factors may not, of course, explain every individual case of crime committed or every individual criminal, but these factors locate criminology squarely in the domain of the social rather than in the domain of individual psychology. It is important to note that this text will also presume that it is social rather than psychological or biological explanations of lawbreaking behaviour which constitute the prime concern of criminology. The implications of this position are twofold and are interconnected.

First, it implies that we shall not be concerned in the following chapters with recent developments of criminological interest which have put to the fore genetic, hormonal, dietary or more general biological factors as the cause of lawbreaking behaviour. This book will presume that such factors are largely irrelevant in explaining the *patterning* of crime. In other words, if we take lawbreaking behaviour as the starting point of criminological concerns it is difficult to see how hormones or genetics can carry information about (changing, social) laws, and thus constitute a meaningful level at which to explain crime.

A further reason for the irrelevance of biological factors is connected with the second implication of foregrounding the social as the arena in which criminological debate is most meaningfully constituted. That lies in understanding the relationship between criminology and criminal justice policy.

Before this is discussed in more detail, however, it will be of value to appreciate some additional criminological 'facts'. One of the features of criminology which has characterized its changing concerns since the mid-1970s has been its increasing focus on criminal victimization. So having said something about what it is that is known about crime it will be useful to say something about what it is that is known about criminal victimization.

What is known about criminal victimization?

The concern with and for the victim of crime has been given greater political and academic prominence since the mid-1970s. Miers (1978) argues that this 'politicization of the victim' was inherent in the formation of the Criminal Injuries Compensation Board in 1964 though it has become many times stronger since then. Such a concern with the victim of crime can be explained in a number of different ways. Certainly the emergence of support services for crime victims in the form of Victim Support (which received its first Home Office funding in the mid-1980s and has been arguably the most rapidly expanding area of the voluntary sector since the late 1970s) provided a voice for the victim of crime where none existed before. In a different way the first and subsequent use of the criminal victimization survey by the Home Office in 1982 also exposed a fuller picture of the nature and extent of criminal victimization than was previously available and contributed in different ways to the growing concern about crime.

Factors such as these, alongside what appeared to be ever failing policies directed towards crime, fuelled the political debate on law and order which consequently increasingly turned its attention to the victim of crime. That attention was concerned not only to highlight the impact of crime on the victim but also to utilize the victim as a resource in combating crime itself. As Karmen (1990) has observed, as a consequence policy, both in the United States and in the UK, became increasingly informed not by crime prevention but by victimization prevention. Informing this general shift in policy has been a growing amount of data on criminal victimization.

The criminal victimization survey has been an important resource in identifying key 'facts' about the victim of crime. If that data source was used as the sole source of information about criminal victimization, then it would be possible to assert that not only are young males most often the offenders (the law breakers), but also they are most often the victims of crime. However, such an assertion would be misleading since it reflects a concern with only one form of lawbreaking behaviour taking place in only one set of circumstances.

If we extend our victimological gaze from the street to the bedroom, to the kitchen and to the workplace, then the picture of who the victims of crime are changes. Women feature much more significantly as victims of crime than do young males. Taking this victimological fact seriously is also a 'truth' which any criminological explanation should consider.

To summarize: criminology as a discipline has been characterized historically by the desire to search for a universal explanation of crime. That search has produced knowledge from a range of disparate starting points, all of which make competing claims in understanding crime. Those competing claims have frequently contributed to the confusion and fuzziness which surrounds the discipline itself. Nevertheless there are some central tenets of criminology around which there is some consensus among academics even if those tenets conflict with more common sense understandings and more emotive political assertions. That consensus is a rather tenuous empirical one more than it is a theoretical one, however. In other words, criminologists *might* agree that the lawbreaking behaviour of young males constitutes one of the key issue of concern, but they will not necessarily agree on what underlying factors result in that concern or what it is that can be done about it. It is at this point that the relationship between criminology, criminal justice policy, and politics referred to earlier re-emerges.

Criminology, politics and criminal justice policy

As Garland (1985) has lucidly argued, criminology as an area of study has always been closely connected to the formation of criminal justice policy. As has been argued elsewhere, this connection can be attributed for the most part to the dominance within criminology (and other social science disciplines) of one particular version of the knowledge gathering and construction process: positivism. The influence of positivism on criminology has been well documented (see, for example, Taylor *et al.*, 1973; Roshier, 1989). One aspect of that influence was felt in the drive to assert a 'positive' influence over the processes of social change that were taking place during the eighteenth and nineteenth centuries. That drive tied criminology to the policy making process as government extended its sphere of influence over social life and took an increasingly directive role in endeavouring to control the impact of social change. Social policies, including criminal justice policies, were formulated against this backcloth resulting in an intimate relationship between the contemporary state of criminological knowledge and the formation of criminal justice policy.

Obviously, the kind of criminological knowledge which has influenced policy formation has varied historically. Some of that knowledge has led to policies which have focused on individual differences and deficiencies whether biological or psychological. More recently, however, policy has been informed by an orientation which has been more generally social in character. Those orientations may, of course, vary in the assumptions they make about human beings and their potential. Our focus here will be to try to unpick some of the general features of criminal justice policy since the late 1970s and to map some of the connections to be made between these features and criminology which will be developed in subsequent chapters. The question might be raised, of course, why since the late 1970s?

The following two quotations (cited in Brake and Hale, 1992: 1) offer one starting point in formulating an answer to this question.

> The most disturbing threat to our freedom and security is the growing disrespect for the rule of law. In government and in opposition, Labour have undermined it . . . The number of crimes in England and Wales is nearly half as much again as it was in 1973. The next Conservative government will spend more on fighting crime even while we economise elsewhere . . . Britain needs strong efficient police forces with high morale.
>
> (Conservative Party Election Manifesto, 1979)

> The origins of crime lie deep in society: in families where parents do not control their children; in schools where discipline is poor; and in the wider world where violence is glamorised and traditional values are under attack. Government *alone* cannot tackle such deep-rooted problems easily or quickly.
>
> (Conservative Party Election Manifesto, 1987)

In citing these two statements Brake and Hale (1992) go on to say that, 'In one sense, law and order can be seen as the Conservative confidence trick of the 1980s, yet, in another it was an integral part of their success'. In some respects Brake and Hale are correct in this assertion. However, perhaps what is of more central concern here is not the way in which the Conservative Party won successive elections but the way in which questions relating to crime, and law and order, were formulated in that process.

As the quote from the Conservative Election Manifesto of 1979 implies, questions relating to law and order in the 1980s were formulated against a backcloth of what were considered to be the earlier political failures of the left. It was certainly the case that the Labour government had struggled with the economic conditions of the mid-1970s which culminated in what was called the 'winter of discontent' of 1978–9. In the area of criminal justice policy in particular there had emerged a sense that 'nothing works' in combating crime. These were among the factors which in some respects made it relatively easy for the Conservative Party to promise a strong stance on law and order which ran tackling street crime and tackling the power of the trade unions together as a strategy for dealing with what were seen as both economic and moral problems. Support for dealing with criminal justice issues in this way did not only exist within the Conservative Party, however.

For example, prior to the 1979 election, the Police Federation took out a full page advertisement in all the national newspapers itemizing a criminal justice strategy echoing that of the Conservative Party. As Reiner (1985: 74) argues, 'the advertisements proved to be an investment which reaped handsome dividends', since at the first opportunity the leaders of the Police Federation were called in to see the Prime Minister and were told that the government would implement the full pay awards recommended by the Edmund-Davies committee. This overt politicization of the police has not retained such a sympathetic flavour. Indeed, by the mid-1980s the police were subjected to similar demands for value for money and efficiency as other public sector organizations and by the early 1990s some Chief Constables were making statements overtly challenging government assumptions on the underlying causes of crime. This example highlights the shifting nature of the political domain and the important impact it has had. Another powerful influence, as has been suggested earlier, was and still is the role of the media.

So, perhaps what is significant about focusing a book on criminological theory since 1979 is the explicit collusion (not conspiracy) between key players in the political process to shift the law and order debate in a particular direction. In some respects, what this shift articulated was a view that the key to understanding a whole range of different social problems lay in understanding their production as being a result of inadequate control. In other words it articulated a general view that 'Insufficient checks on the instinctive desires and proclivities which cause people to break the law have led to high crime levels' (Brake and Hale, 1992: 18). So the policies which emanated from the implicit acceptance of this view have been ones which have variously concerned themselves with issues from tougher prison regimes to reducing the potential influence of (soft, left wing) police authorities. Moreover, these policies and this general view of the problem of law and order, as being produced as a consequence of inadequate controls, reflect what is called the neoclassical view of crime, discussed in more detail in Chapter 3.

Put simply, this is a view of crime which argues that offenders calculate the costs and benefits of offending before they commit an offence. In policy terms this means that if you make offending more painful, that is, increase the costs, you will reduce the offending behaviour. It is a view of crime which has been at its most influential in the United States through the work of J. Q. Wilson, whose *Thinking about Crime* was published in 1975.

It is a moot point as to the extent to which such academic theorizing underpinned Conservative Party policy in 1979. What is clear, however, is that as the 1980s progressed there emerged a version of what might be called 'Conservative criminology' (that is that kind of criminological 'wisdom' associated with the Conservative Party) which selectively tapped into and utilized variants of 'conservative criminology' (that emanating from academia). At the same time, those more inclined to left wing political and policy thinking were also endeavouring to regenerate the debate on law and order in a form which would shift it away from neoclassicism (this is discussed in greater detail in Chapter 4).

The fervour with which the debate on law and order on both the left and the right proceeded during the 1980s constitutes one reason for examining the particular developments occurring within criminology during that time. The way in which the discipline endeavoured to intervene in that political debate and the way in which the political parties chose to voice some aspects of criminological concern is a valuable path to map. So, while criminology and criminal justice policy have always been intertwined with one another, it is important to develop an appreciation of the complexities of the links between the two, especially in the contemporary context. The chapters which follow will attempt to highlight the complexity of such links.

Conclusion: what then are the key features of criminology?

This introduction has endeavoured to highlight a number of features about criminology.

1 As a discipline it is held together by a substantive concern: crime.
2 This means that it is multidisciplinary in character rather than being dominated by one discipline. As a consequence, in order to make sense of what criminologists might be saying it is important to understand the conceptual apparatus with which they might be working.
3 Thus criminologists frequently disagree with one another.
4 Despite such disagreements, it could be argued that there is some consensus around some features of what constitutes the crime problem though much less agreement on how to 'solve' the crime problem.
5 Nevertheless criminologists have been historically (and still are contemporaneously) concerned to offer some form of intervention in the policy making process.
6 These features of criminology sometimes resonate with popular (common-sense) thinking about crime and sometimes challenge such thinking. Such tensions are a perpetual challenge for the discipline.

These features of criminology render it both stimulating and frustrating as an area of study. They also reflect the more general strengths and weaknesses between theoretical and practical concerns of any applied area of study.

It has already been said that this analysis of criminology is premised on the view that it is at the level of the social that criminology can best formulate an answer to the crime question. What such an answer might look like, however, will be highly dependent on which variables that comprise 'the social' are privileged. In the chapters which follow we shall be examining the different ways in which different strands of criminological thought privilege different variables and concepts in their endeavours both to understand crime, explain crime, and capture the policy domain in order to make a difference to the nature and extent of the crime problem. One of the particular concerns of this book will be to unpick how criminology since 1979 has endeavoured to address the question of 'what works' in the context of preventing and reducing crime and what might constitute the inherent weaknesses in the foundations of the discipline itself which might militate against providing any effective answers to that question.

So, the claims made in the title *Understanding Criminology* are considerable indeed. In some respects there is little agreement about the nature of the subject matter of this area of study, how it might be best studied, how its findings might be best translated into policy, and how that might be achieved. Nevertheless in each of the chapters which follow we shall be concerned to map such competing claims to knowledge and the differential influence they have had.

In order therefore to contextualize the developments which have occurred within criminology since the mid-1970s, Chapter 2 will offer a brief but critical introduction on the nature of criminology, and the competing theoretical perspectives within criminology, prior to that time. In Chapter 3 we shall consider those varieties of 'conservative criminology' which can be found in different ways in right wing thinking about crime. In Chapter 4 we shall consider the emergence of 'left realism' as a response to those ideas. Each of these different ways of theorizing crime display criminology's continued attachment to the modernist project and to the production of an associated policy agenda. It is interesting to note that some of the keenest criticism of 'left realism' has emerged from those working within a postmodernist framework, so it is in Chapter 4 that we shall also consider some features of that critique. Postmodernism emerges as a relevant theme again in Chapter 5, which maps the various ways in which the question of gender has been rendered more or less visible within the criminological enterprise and what questions remain unanswered for a criminology which does not have a gendered lens. Chapters 6 and 7 share a common concern. The view of both of these chapters is that there is much left to be addressed within a criminology with a modernist heart. These chapters argue for a criminology which has at its centre a concern with social justice and they endeavour to demonstrate the extent to which debates about the underclass, for example, or repeat victimization, might be better formulated by a criminology so informed. In conclusion, Chapter 8 offers one way of furthering the conceptual apparatus of a criminology which is willing to engage in a self-reflexive critique of its modernist and gendered presumptions. In that chapter we shall consider the importance to criminology of understanding the concepts of risk, trust, and the underlying relationship between the citizen and the state, as being key to a criminology of the future.

Further reading

A range of textbooks now endeavour to offer a feel for crime as a social problem and the response of criminology to that. Such introductions to the discipline provide a useful foundation not only for more theoretical concerns but also to what it is that criminologists know and do not know. A good example is Felson (1994) *Crime and Everyday Life*. For those wishing to pursue a more detailed understanding of the changing nature and impact of the wider political context and its relationship to criminology, see Brake and Hale (1992) *Public Order and Private Lives*. For the more philosophically inclined, Roshier (1989) *Controlling Crime* provides a sound analysis of positivism and its influence on criminology.

chapter two

Perspectives in criminological theory

It has been established so far that criminology as an area of study is a diverse discipline characterized by competing theoretical perspectives. However, despite this diversity it is an area of study which has always been embedded in policy and the policy making process. This central feature of the discipline informs the developments which have occurred within criminology since 1979. However, before we proceed to examine those developments, it will be useful to identify some of the key themes embedded in earlier criminological debate. Consequently it will be possible to understand the legacy of those themes for more contemporary theorizing and the ways in which that legacy informs present debates.

It is possible to identify three recurrent themes within criminological theory which will be labelled here as a concern with the *behaviour of criminals*, a concern with the *criminality of behaviour*, and a concern with the *criminality of the state*. Each of these themes has been more or less popular at different historical moments and each directs the criminological agenda, in theory and in practice, in quite different ways. We shall discuss each of them in turn.

The behaviour of criminals

A focus on the behaviour of criminals directs our attention to a central concern with the individual and the role of individual differences in producing crime. As Chapter 1 suggested, different writers have endeavoured to construct different historical connections for the emergence of criminology as a discipline. If a broad view of that history is constructed, a concern with the behaviour of individual criminals can be traced to early religious talk about crime. That view implied that criminals were possessed by demons and as a consequence they were subjected to different kinds of trials to rid them of such influences. For some religious sects, this way of thinking about crime is still considered to be appropriate today. Here, however, we shall be concerned primarily with two different ways of thinking about the individual behaviour of criminals, the classical school of thought, and the positivist school of thought. Both of these have a resonance with the later criminological concerns discussed in Chapters 4 and 5.

Classical criminology

The key feature of classical criminology is its central presumption that individual criminals engage in a process of rational calculative decision making in choosing how to commit crime. This view is underpinned by two further assumptions: one that individuals have free will; the other that individuals are guided by hedonism, the maximization of pleasure and the minimization of pain. These ideas, in their initial formulation, were important in that they shifted attention towards punishing the offensive behaviour rather than 'punishing' the individual's social or physical characteristics in and of themselves. This shift consequently had an enormous influence on changing attitudes towards punishment and towards the purpose of the law and the legal system.

Classical ideas about crime and punishment can be found in the works of a number of different writers. The writings of Beccaria (1738–94) and Bentham (1748–1832), however, were especially influential. Of the two, Beccaria is frequently cited as being most influential in the subsequent development of the criminological agenda.

Put simply, Beccaria argued that there was a contractual relationship between the individual and the state. This relationship existed to prevent chaos. As a part of this contractual relationship individuals gave up some of their liberties in the interest of the common good with the purpose of the law to ensure that these common interests were met. For Beccaria, this meant that the law should be limited in scope and written down so that people could make decisions on how to behave. Importantly punishment was to fit the crime, not the individual, and was to be certain and swift. Offenders were to be seen as reasonable people with the same capacity for resisting offending behaviour as non-offenders. The guiding principle of the criminal justice process, it was argued, was the presumption of innocence; and in this general framework punishment was to be seen as a deterrent to criminal behaviour. The central concern of the law and the criminal justice process was therefore the prevention of crime through this deterrent function.

These ideas were very influential in reforming criminal codes and informing legislative changes in a number of different social contexts. They were particularly influential in France at the time of the French Revolution and, it is argued, informed the formulation of the American Constitution. However, despite the significant ways in which these ideas underpinned major changes in different legal frameworks, these changes did not accommodate the issue of children's criminal behaviour and did not solve the rising crime rate. Crime was still becoming increasingly problematic. Consequently, as social conditions worsened for many sections of different societies subsequent to the Industrial Revolution, the idea of individuals being motivated by hedonism and free will lost some of its popularity. In its place a more determined image of the human being was constructed. This image reflected one of the ideas which contributed to the birth of positivism within criminology.

Positivist criminology

Many reviews of the development of criminology begin with reference to the influence of positivism. While the specific meaning to be attached to this term is open to some debate, in the context of criminology it is usually used to refer to a scientific commitment to the gathering of the 'facts' which cause crime. It is this search for 'facts' which most clearly delineates one of the differences between this version of criminology and classical criminology. The other main difference between these two different versions of the criminal individual was the commitment of the early positivists especially to search for the cause of crime within individual biology rather than individual free will. Lombroso (1853–1909) is frequently considered to be the Founding Father of this version of criminological thought.

Lombroso's ideas about crime are clearly influenced by the work of Darwin. The ideas of evolution, which so challenged religious principles of the nineteenth century, are embedded in the work of Lombroso. Most easily identified as an anthropologist, Lombroso embraced what was referred to as the law of biogenetics. This law articulated a particular view of evolutionary development in which it is posited that every individual organism revisits the developmental history of its own species type within its own individual history. The phrase 'ontology recapitulates phylogeny' captured this view of the developmental process and introduced an important concept, that of recapitulation, to Lombrosian criminology. The idea that every living organism, as it develops, undergoes each stage of its own species history, provided

a mechanism for explaining both the normal and the abnormal (the patho-
logical). This was achieved through the related concept of atavism.

It was clear, even to those committed to Darwin's ideas, that every individual member of a species type did not always possess all the characteristics
of that species type; in other words, abnormalities were produced from time
to time. These abnormalities, it was argued, were a product of that individual member being a throwback to an earlier stage of the developmental
history of the species: that is, atavistic. In this way the concept of atavism
permitted the law of biogenetics to retain its universal status; aberrations
were explained as being reversions to an earlier species type. The idea of
atavism appealed to the criminal anthropologists, especially Lombroso.

Lombroso assumed that the process of recapitulation usually produced
normal individuals. Someone who became criminal, therefore, must constitute a throwback to an earlier stage of biological development – an atavistic
degeneration. For Lombroso, such biological degenerations manifested
themselves in the peculiar physical attributes possessed by criminals: sloping
foreheads, receding chins, excessively long arms, unusual ear size, and so on,
resulting in the view of the 'born criminal'.

This commitment to the biological origin of criminal behaviour led Lombroso to construct a fourfold typology of criminals: the born criminal (true
atavistic types); the insane criminal (including those suffering from a range
of mental illnesses); the occasional criminal (opportunist criminals who
commit crime because they possess innate traits which propel them in that
direction); and criminals of passion (who commit crime as a result of some
irresistible force). For all of these criminal types, their behaviour is a result
of their abnormality, that is determined by forces out of their control, rather
than the consequence of freely chosen action.

The legacy of Lombrosian criminology has been profound. While the
notion of the 'born criminal' might appear somewhat simple and naive in the
late twentieth century, Lombroso's commitment to a science of the criminal,
and the search for a universal explanation of crime located within the individual, laid the foundation for much of the criminological work which came
after. Moreover, the search for the cause of crime within the individual and
individual differences continued albeit focusing on different biological and
or psychological factors. This has ranged from work on heredity (Goring,
1913), to body type (Kretschmer, 1926), to the notion of a criminal personality (Eysenck and Gudjonnson, 1990).

Latterly, this way of thinking about crime has become theoretically more
sophisticated in the form of the biosocial theory of Wilson and Herrnstein
(1985) discussed in Chapter 5, and has become technologically more complex in the increasingly controversial world of neuroscience. Here, using
advanced technology to construct images of the brain, the view that individuals are merely negatives waiting to be developed, is beginning to reopen

the whole debate about whether or not human beings possess free will and where and how an understanding of criminal behaviour might be situated within that debate. Thus the tension remains between classical and positivist views on the nature of human beings.

Each of these versions of focusing on the behaviour of the criminal carries with them different policy implications. As was suggested earlier for the classical criminologist, if individuals had a calculative, hedonistic approach to crime, then the purpose of the criminal justice system was to punish in order to deter them from committing crime. For the positivist, on the other hand, if an individual's criminal behaviour was to be understood as being determined by their biological and/or psychological make-up the purpose of the criminal justice system is either to incapacitate them or, if appropriate, offer them treatment until they were no longer a threat to society. In more current policy debate the influence of these different ways of thinking about and using the criminal justice system are still evident, standing as some testimony to the importance of these ideas.

Positivistic approaches to explaining crime were to be found not only within the search for the individual roots of criminal behaviour, but also in much more sociologically informed approaches to criminology. These approaches take as their focus of concern the wider socio-economic and cultural conditions which may or may not propel individuals into criminal behaviour and it is these more sociologically informed approaches we shall consider under our next thematic heading: a concern with the criminality of behaviour.

The criminality of behaviour

A concern with the criminality of behaviour focuses attention on factors external to the individual which might result in their behaviour either being lawbreaking or being defined as lawbreaking. These ways of thinking about crime have also been influenced by positivism in the sense that they are approaches which have been equally concerned to identify the 'facts' which result in criminality. The way in which that concern has been addressed can be discussed in a number of different ways. For the purposes of this discussion three central ideas can be identified: the concept of social disorganization, strain theory and its derivatives, and labelling theory.

Social disorganization

The concept of social disorganization emanates from the Chicago School of sociology of the 1920s and 1930s. It reflects one of two main strands of theoretical work coming out of Chicago which were to influence quite profoundly the later development of both criminology and the sociology of deviance, namely, social ecology and symbolic interactionism. Symbolic interactionism is discussed on pp. 24–26. The concept of social disorganization is associated with those theorists concerned to understand the social ecology of the city.

Social ecologists drew parallels between the way in which it was thought living organisms maintained themselves and the maintenance of social life. In other words, just as it was possible to identify patterns in the processes of development and adaptation to the environment in the animal and plant world so it was possible to identify similar patterns in the growth and development of the city. This led theorists to suggest that it made sense to think of the city as a series of concentric zones radiating from the city centre: with each zone having different social and economic characteristics and the people living in those different areas differently adapting to those social circumstances. These general presumptions, when overlaid on the substantive data available about city life, led to a much more detailed appreciation of these differing patterns of adaptation. In particular, attention was focused on the 'zone of transition', the area nearest the city centre.

The 'zone of transition' became the focal concern since this was the area in which new immigrants to the city settled (as it was inexpensive and near to places of work), but it was also the area which appeared to manifest more social problems (according to official statistics) from incidences of ill health to crime. The manifestation of problems such as these is explained by the social ecologists as being the result of the breakdown of primary social relationships in this area, with the highly mobile and transitory nature of social life breeding impersonality and fragmentation.

In general terms, then, this theoretical perspective is suggesting that the processes of industrialization and urbanization create communities in which, as a result of immigration and subsequent migration, there are competing norms and values, the consequence of which is the breakdown of traditional norms and values: social disorganization. It is within this general context that crime is most likely to occur. Through the notion of cultural transmission it was also argued that these modes of adaptation to different social conditions in the city were likely to be passed on from one generation to the next as new immigrants enter that part of the city and adapt to those social conditions.

This way of thinking about and explaining the patterning of criminal behaviour (as it was officially recorded) was one of the first to consider the social origins of criminality as opposed to the individual roots of crime. As a result, it not only influenced subsequent generations of sociologically informed criminological work, but also carries with it clear policy implications. In theoretical terms, the concept of social disorganization led later theorists to work in different ways with the interaction between social structure and the social production of norms and values. In policy terms, it has led to a focus on how to reorganize socially disorganized communities, to understanding the ways in which the environment might contribute to crime (designing out crime), and to a concern with how general neighbourhood decline (rising incivilities) might contribute to the crime career of a community, to name several recurring and contemporarily relevant policy themes. It is clear that the focus on the way in which social conditions produce social pathology is a common thread between the social ecologists and those who took up the ideas of strain theory.

Strain theory

Strain theory emanates primarily from the work of Robert Merton (1938, 1968). His theoretical work was concerned more with the way in which the tensions between the legitimate and illegitimate means of acceding to the norms and values of a particular society resulted in deviant (rather than just criminal) behaviour. The influence of these ideas on criminology have been profound. Merton's ideas can be situated within the theoretical tradition of functionalism. Largely informed by the work of Émile Durkheim and Talcott Parsons, functionalism views society rather like a finely tuned biological organism. In order for society to work effectively its component parts must be in balance and there must be some consensus or agreement concerning the appropriateness of that balance. Put simply, this balance produces social order. Any imbalance results in social disorder.

Merton's work endeavoured to address the social and cultural norms and values which underpinned social order and/or disorder. Centrally he was concerned to identify the circumstances in which, while there might be socially approved ways of achieving success, not everyone by definition had access to those socially approved means, so how did those who lacked such opportunities adapt to the strain which that produced?

In order to understand the conflict generated between acceptance of the norms and values of mainstream society and the ability to succeed within those norms and values, Merton constructed a fivefold typology. This typology was intended to capture, schematically, those people who accepted the cultural norms and values and the institutionalized means of achieving those norms and values (the conformists) to those people who rejected both and put new ones in their place (the rebellious). This schema was intended to convey the ways in which the structure of society in and of itself produced deviant behaviour, some of which would also be criminal behaviour, at all levels in the social structure.

However, the primary implications of this schema resulted in a focus on those in the lower classes since, given the strains of their structural location, it was presumed that they were the most likely to engage in non-conformist behaviour. There are two important theoretical developments which arguably follow on from Merton's concern with the production of deviant behaviour: Cohen's notion of the delinquent subculture and Cloward and Ohlin's concept of differential opportunity. This focus on the lower classes constitutes one of the common strands between Merton's theoretical work and those who came after. We shall discuss each of these in turn.

Cohen's book *Delinquent Boys* was published in 1955. Drawing on both Merton's work and the notion of cultural transmission embedded within social disorganization theory, Cohen developed a framework in which to understand why delinquent subcultures seemed to be formed primarily within deprived inner city areas. Cohen's argument, following Merton, was that lower class youth strove to embrace the norms and values of main-stream society but lacked the means to achieve success. They thus suffered from status frustration: they were denied the status of respectability because they did not have the means to achieve such respectability. Delinquent sub-culture provided an alternative, sometimes oppositional, means of achieving such status. So the strains produced as a consequence of social disorganiza-tion result in the formation of norms and values through which lower class youth can achieve status and success.

One question, however, remained unanswered within this framework; how was it that not all lower class youth embraced the delinquent subcul-ture nor chose the same kind of deviant solution despite being subjected to similar strains of social disorganization? It is at this point that the notion of differential opportunity structures associated with the work of Cloward and Ohlin (1960) became important.

Again embracing Mertonian strain theory, Cloward and Ohlin argued that there is more than one way in any society to achieve success. There are both legitimate and illegitimate pathways. In their view the upper and middle classes have greater access to the legitimate opportunity structure, with the lower classes having greater access to the illegitimate opportunity structure. In a community where these two different kinds of opportunity structures are poorly integrated, there tends to be greater social disorgani-zation. The greater the social disorganization, the more likely that the illegitimate opportunity structure, especially organized criminal gangs, will become dominant. This kind of opportunity structure, it was suggested, pro-vides an alternative route for status and success for those who join it.

Cloward and Ohlin's theory facilitates an understanding of the ways in which different kinds of delinquent subcultures come to be prevalent in different kinds of urban locations; from the retreatist gang (those primarily engaged in drugs), to the conflict gang (those most concerned with violence), the variable factor which predicts which outcome being the level of inte-gration between the different opportunity structures. Thus rather like Cohen, Cloward and Ohlin were endeavouring to weave together the work of the Chicago School on social disorganization with the strain theory of Robert Merton.

What strain theory, and its derivatives achieved, was to centre the importance of structural variables, external to the individual, as a way of understanding the nature of criminal behaviour. What Cohen and Cloward and Ohlin were concerned to address was the question of subculture. They accepted the Mertonian proposition that some people were disadvantaged in their efforts to achieve success and what required explanation was the resulting deviant behaviour. These conditions were mediated by the formation of different subcultural responses. This focus on the interrelationship between structural condition and subcultural response still has current resonance. Some would argue that the ultimate testing ground for this relationship lies within the more current concerns and debates on the underclass (see Chapter 6). Understanding the relevance of subculture is not solely the preserve of those on the right. It is also a concern of those on the left (see Chapter 4). In the 1960s this work certainly laid the groundwork for the further development of a second strand of thought emanating from the Chicago School. That work, largely associated with symbolic interactionism, placed much greater emphasis on the social processes involved in becoming deviant and came to be called labelling theory.

Labelling theory

Labelling theory returns us to the second school of thought which characterized the Chicago School of sociology during the 1920s and 1930s: symbolic interactionism. Originating with the work of George Herbert Mead, symbolic interactionists were concerned to understand the processes underpinning social life and the mechanisms by which meanings are assigned to those processes. As a theoretical perspective, symbolic interactionism centres the creative capacities of human beings and their ability to share understandings with one another. These general propositions direct attention towards the quality of the interactions which take place between people, how those interactions are understood, and how they become modified, refined and developed. This perspective, then, shares common concerns with strain theory in addressing the general question of how behaviour comes to be understood as deviant (rather than criminal) and the role of shared norms and values in that process. In this latter respect the work of Howard Becker, with what came to be called labelling theory, has been particularly influential.

There are two strands to Becker's (1963) labelling theory: a concern to address how it is that a particular behaviour is labelled as deviant, and a concern to understand the impact of that labelling process. As Becker states:

> Social groups create deviance by making the rules whose infraction constitutes deviance, and by applying those rules to particular people and labelling them as outsiders. From this point of view, deviance is not a quality of the act the person commits, but rather a consequence of the

application by others of rules and sanctions to an 'offender'. The deviant is one to whom that label has been successfully applied; deviant behaviour is behaviour that people so label.

(Becker, 1963: 9)

In understanding deviance, then, importance lies with the reaction to the behaviour not the behaviour itself. This led Becker to construct a fourfold typology of possible labels (reactions) to perceived deviant behaviour: the falsely accused, the pure deviant, the conformist, and the secret deviant.

This focus on the labelling process led criminologists and sociologists to think about criminal behaviour in quite a different way. For instance, while officially recorded crime data identified young, lower class males as the key criminal group, labelling theorists wanted to explore what it was about the criminal justice agencies that led them to focus attention on this particular group of people (as opposed to others who might be secretly deviant, that is, not publicly labelled as deviant). Others became more concerned with the impact of being labelled deviant and explored the notion of a deviant career.

Labelling theory had a major impact on criminology, questioning the disciplines primarily middle class assumptions about the processes surrounding crime and criminal behaviour which led to a closer examination of the way in which the criminal justice system operates and processes individuals. In policy terms, it connects most directly with diversionary policies and initiatives of decriminalization; that is with those policies concerned to divert (potential) offenders from crime and/or the criminal justice system.

But, both in theory and in practice, labelling theory has its limitations, perhaps best summarized by Sumner:

it is equally problematic that 'labelling theorists' (1) never specified in detail the ideological constitution of the moral and criminal categories, (2) never fully explored the links between these categories and the social structure, and (3) only dealt with the relationship between moral/legal condemnation and 'interest' in an instrumental way.

(Sumner, 1990: 23)

The key problem which is embedded in these observations made by Sumner is the question of power and power relationships.

Underpinning the theoretical strands of thought discussed here is a common image of society. That image presumes, for the most part, the normatively predominant view of society as comprising a democratic and consensual process. Largely as a consequence of this presumption, attention is implicitly focused on those who deviate from this normative view, which for the most part results in a concern with the deviant and/or criminal behaviour of the lower classes. There is, however, an alternative way of thinking about the nature of society, which results in quite a different focus in relation to thinking about crime. That view is subsumed in the third theme to be discussed here – the criminality of the state.

The criminality of the state

There is a clear connection between a critical analysis of labelling processes and their impact and the development of a close interest in those who have the power to label. However, once theorists were moved to consider the question of power and power relationships, it also became clear that the implicit view of society previously held could not accommodate these newer concerns. In theoretical terms it made much more sense to turn to Marx and a view of society as rooted in conflicting interests than to retain the Parsonian image of consensus.

General Marxist presumptions about the nature of society direct attention to the way in which the powerful in society use the various resources available to them (including the law) to secure and maintain their dominant position. In particular, then, this means that the law and the processes which underpin the formation of the law are placed under scrutiny, alongside the way in which the law is used to criminalize particular social groups in the interests of the powerful. Consequently the law, and its enforcement, are seen as particular sites where the legitimized powers of the state are exercised. Those powers, it is argued, express themselves especially along class, race and gender lines.

There are a number of different writers whose work can be located under this general heading of concern with the criminality of the state. Here particular attention will be paid to three varieties of this interest: Marxist criminology, radical criminology, and critical criminology. While these labels certainly are not mutually exclusive, the ideas associated with each of them will be discussed in turn.

Marxist criminology

Strands of Marxist theorizing can be found in the writings of various criminologists. Arguably the work of Chambliss (1975) and Quinney (1977) has been particularly influential.

Chambliss' work is a clear attempt to use Marxist theorizing to construct a political economy of crime. Marx himself had little to say about crime or the law, but the general tenor of his views on society and social relationships can be translated into the criminological context. As Chambliss argues, capitalism creates the desire to consume and it has to be recognized that not all members of society are able to earn enough to match the levels of consumption induced by the capitalist process. There are the owners and the non-owners, the bourgeoisie and the proletariat, all of whom have different capacities at different points in time both to produce and to consume.

Moreover, the underlying logical development of the capitalist process, it is argued, inevitably results in more and more situations where those who have and those who do not are put in conflict with one another. Sometimes that conflict is violent; more often it results in the behaviour of those who do not have being labelled as criminal. Thus for Chambliss

> The criminal law is thus not a reflection of custom . . . but a set of rules laid down by the state in the interests of the ruling class, and resulting from the conflicts that inhere in class structured societies; criminal behaviour is, then, the inevitable expression of class conflict resulting from the inherently exploitative nature of economic relations.
>
> (Chambliss, 1975, abridged in Muncie *et al.*, 1996: 225)

In this sense, then, crime is to be understood as a reaction to the general life conditions in which individuals find themselves as a result of their social class position.

Within this general framework, of course, there is no necessary presumption that only the relatively powerless are likely to engage in criminal activities. Indeed the general proposition would be that all people in all social classes are capable of committing crime. What is central to this argument is understanding why only some behaviours are so targeted as criminal. To quote Chambliss (1975) again

> Criminality is simply not something that people have or don't have; crime is not something some people do and others don't. Crime is a matter of who can pin the label on whom, and underlying this socio-political process is the structure of social relations determined by the political economy.
>
> (abridged in Muncie *et al.*, 1996: 228)

So for Chambliss the underlying cause of crime lies not with individuals, or their greater or lesser acceptance of cultural norms and values, it lies with the state and the political and economic interests which are necessarily served by the law and its implementation.

In some respects, there is still a rational image of the human being embedded in this theoretical framework offered by Chambliss. Crime is to be seen as a rational response to social conditions for some individuals. It is a way of managing the material reality of their lives. This is a variation on the observation made by Marx, that men make choices but not in circumstances of their own choosing. This rationality is consequently circumscribed. It is not the rationality of free will but that which is rationally dictated by the political economy of social relations. As Chambliss argues, 'The state becomes an instrument of the ruling class enforcing laws here but not there, according to the realities of political power and economic conditions' (abridged in Muncie *et al.*, 1996: 230). A similar theoretical feel is found in the work of Quinney (1977).

It can be argued that Quinney's ideas were equally influenced by the work of the phenomenologists as they were by Marx. Consequently different readings of his work can and do emphasize these different theoretical inputs. In general terms, however, Quinney talked about the 'politicality of law' and the 'politicality of crime'. By the politicality of law, Quinney was referring to the extent to which social relations are reflected in the law and the law making process. Social relations which rendered some issues visible and ensured that others remained invisible, in other words reflected political interests.

In talking about the politicality of crime, Quinney was referring to criminal behaviour as a 'conscientious' activity; not the produce of poor socialization or a deficient personality, but a political expression. In other words, it is not the behaviour which is criminal but the action which is taken against it which renders it criminal.

There is a particular view of society which underlies these twin concerns. This view of society emphasizes the social construction of social reality. In its extreme form, this view of society presumes that social reality is simply a reflection of an individual's state of mind. In its milder versions it is intended to draw attention to the way in which our understanding of social, political and criminological issues (to name a few) are constantly subject to changing perceptions and interpretations. This latter theme links Quinney's general theoretical framework with that of critical criminology (discussed on pp. 30–2).

In this particular context, however, Quinney was endeavouring to draw attention to the ways in which definitions of what is and what is not problematic become taken for granted and embedded in social relations, a process which serves the interests of the powerful much more readily than it serves the interests of the powerless. This, he argued, was a structural rather than a conspiratorial relationship.

Quinney went on to construct a typology of crime which could form the central focus of a criminology informed by these ideas. In this typology he talks of crime of domination (police brutality, white collar crime, governmental crimes), crimes of accommodation and resistance (theft and homicide produced by the conditions of capitalism) and terrorism (a response to the conditions of capitalism). Essentially this position reflects a view of the causality of crime as being an expression of the desire for social change, that is, as a political act.

Both of these versions of criminology have two themes in common. Put simply, they both see crime as a product of the behaviour of the authorities rather than as a product of individuals. In other words, this kind of Marxist theorizing endeavours to further the labelling perspective's concern with the power to label. In addition, they both see crime as a relative phenomenon rather than an absolute one. In other words, there is nothing inherently wicked or sinful in criminal behaviour; it is simply behaviour that is so targeted.

The policy implications of work informed in this way are clearly neither simple nor straightforward. They ultimately imply a different social and economic order. Indeed in many respects little practical work ensued from these theoretical developments as a consequence. However, these ideas were valuable in drawing criminological attention to the role of the law in defining the criminality that is seen and not seen and in establishing a much sharper critical focus on those processes. Moreover, these general ideas were also influential in contributing to what has been called here radical criminology, the next theme to be discussed here.

Radical criminology

The radical criminology of Taylor *et al.* (1973), which will form the basis of the discussion here, did not emerge in a vacuum. Though largely taken as the starting point of more radical work in the UK, the ideas contained within *The New Criminology* had their origins in the work of earlier labelling theorists as well as versions of Marxist criminology (discussed above). This work remains influential largely because it was one of the first to offer a wide ranging critique of the (then) dominant form of criminology. This dominant form was peopled mostly by psychologists and psychiatrists, concerned with the behaviour of the criminal, looking for the cause of crime within the individual.

Taylor, Walton and Young not only provided a thoroughgoing critique of criminology, but also endeavoured to offer a theoretical perspective to replace this focus on the individual with a focus on the social construction of crime. In so doing they offered a theory synthesizing labelling theory with Marxism as a means of retaining a concern with the value of appreciating individual meaning and action (the question of authenticity) alongside the power of state agencies to control and define (the question of the role of the state). It will be valuable to examine this framework in a little more detail.

The New Criminology has seven elements to it. The first argues that in order to understand a crime (or a deviant act) it is important to locate that act within wider social processes. In other words, individual behaviour must be placed in a wider social, political and economic context. There must be a political economy of crime. Second, having situated a behaviour in this way, sight should not be lost of the immediate circumstances and origins of criminal behaviour. In other words, how and why individuals choose to respond to their structural location in the way that they do, which is expressed as a requirement for a social psychology of crime. Third, people may choose to behave in a particular way, but may for various reasons not carry out their choices or their choices may become modified in the process of interaction. Recognition of these processes means that it is necessary to offer an account of the social dynamics of crime; what were the interactive processes which led to one outcome rather than another?

Fourth, people may behave in a range of different ways, some of which may be labelled deviant some of which may not be, irrespective of the behaviour itself. In other words, it is important to understand the social reaction to crime. That social reaction may be rooted in the social psychology of what passes between the witnesses to a particular behaviour but it may also be located in a wider audience. That wider audience will include professionals working in the criminal justice agencies as well as other people significant to the offender. Their response to different behaviours requires an understanding of what Taylor *et al.* call a political economy of social reaction – the fifth proposition. The sixth concern is with the relationship between the social reaction to the deviant and/or criminal behaviour and the impact of that social reaction. In other words, how might this impact or not on their future criminal careers?

The final characteristic or proposition of what these authors call a fully social theory of deviance constitutes an implicit acceptance of the dialectical nature of social reality.

> The central requirement of a fully social theory of deviance, however, is that these formal requirements must not be treated simply as essential factors all of which need to be present (in invariant fashion) if the theory is to be social. Rather it is that these formal requirements must all appear in the theory, as they do in the real world, in a complex, dialectical relationship to one another.
>
> (Taylor *et al.*, 1973, abridged in Muncie *et al.*, 1996: 237)

This last requirement demands that account be taken of the nature of the criminal process as a whole and how its component parts produce the whole.

Thus this version of talking about the criminality of the state, while offering a differently nuanced theoretical emphasis from that which was to be found in Marxist criminology *per se*, certainly shares in some of its concerns. In particular, as a result of the emphasis that these theoretical concerns placed on understanding the processes of criminalization, it certainly served to challenge the individualistic correctional stance of earlier criminologies. It also laid the foundation for later theoretical developments, particularly from those wishing to pursue the differing ways in which the power associated with the political economy of the state asserts itself. This is the central focus of the last of the themes to be discussed here – critical criminology.

Critical criminology

The use of the label 'critical' is employed by different writers intending to invoke differing frames of analysis. It is used here to identify those who have concerned themselves with the multiplicity of way in which the state deploys its use of power. The work of Foucault has been very influential in encouraging a more careful and detailed analysis of the concept of power and how power is asserted. Foucault was particularly interested in the ways in which knowledge and power are constituted in each other, and especially interested in the ways in which this mutual interdependence effectively exercised social control (Foucault, 1977). In some respects, then, critical criminology is concerned to unravel the ways in which taken for granted talk about social problems both simultaneously serves to define those problems and control them. In this sense its focus stems not only from the work of Foucault but also from those of a more traditional Marxist persuasion for whom the state is more explicitly implicated in rendering some issues visible and others invisible. Critical criminology seeks to develop this concern in a more subtly nuanced fashion.

Put simply, critical criminology seeks to explore the ways in which the variables of class, race and gender are played out in the criminal justice system. This version of criminology argues that each of these variables differently articulate a different structural relationship with the interests of the state. This is more than just a concern with the (potential) for discriminatory practices. It reflects a concern with the ideas which underpin discriminatory practices and consequently contribute to their perpetuation: how they become institutionalized. As Scraton and Chadwick state:

> Once institutionalised, however, classism, sexism, heterosexism, and racism become systemic and structured. They become the taken for granted social histories and contemporary priorities which constitute state institutions, informing policies and underwriting practices, and which provide legitimacy to interpersonal discrimination. Through the process of institutionalisation, relations of dominance and subjugation achieve structural significance.
>
> (Scraton and Chadwick, 1991: 168)

This position, therefore, not only reflects a concern with the myriad of mechanisms whereby the state reaffirms its power and the underlying structural relations which support that power, as the quote above implies in its more recent affirmation critical criminology also centres the relationship between structure and agency as found in the work of Giddens (1984). In the same article, Scraton and Chadwick go on to state that

> What this discussion has pursued is the central argument that critical criminology recognises the reciprocity inherent in the relationship between structure and agency but also that structural relations embody the primary determining contexts of production, reproduction and neo-colonialism.
>
> (Scraton and Chadwick, 1991: 166)

These contexts do not determine outcome. That is the product of the complex interplay between structure and agency in which neither are human beings seen as the sole determiners of what it is that they can and cannot do or how it is that they are seen and not seen. This use of the term critical is certainly redolent of the way in which it has been used in more recent victimological concerns which are discussed in Chapter 7.

Critical criminology, then, is concerned to unpick the ways in which ideas which support the state and state practices serve to marginalize and consequently criminalize some groups and not others. In addition it represents a set of theoretical ideas designed to situate the significance of history to these processes. Of particular importance is the way in which this theoretical perspective centres the questions of not only class but also race and gender. In this latter respect it constitutes an important development from the radical criminology of Taylor, Walton and Young of 1973.

As can be seen, the notion of the criminality of the state shifts the criminological agenda away from seeing society as essentially consensual towards seeing society as essentially rooted in conflict. This fundamental shift not only locates the explanation of crime squarely in the social domain, it also centres the practices of the powerful, both the seen and the unseen, as legitimate concerns for the criminological agenda.

This shift in concern also seriously challenges the previously unchallenged presumption contained within much criminological work: the fundamental belief in the objectivity of knowledge. One common thread between those seeking to address the criminality of the state is the implied critique of this view of knowledge and the knowledge production process. In general terms within this perspective, knowledge is understood much more meaningfully as ideology – ideology which more or less supports the state and its practices. This view of knowledge seriously challenges the hold of positivism on criminology. It is a hold which is nevertheless still present and still significant in the criminological debates which have followed.

There are clearly some quite significant variations in the way in which this focus on the criminality of the state has been expressed as this discussion has demonstrated. These variations notwithstanding, the importance of these concerns have remained relevant, if differently developed in more contemporary theorising. Indeed, it was against the backcloth of these theoretical developments, perhaps rather pejoratively labelled by Young as 'left idealism', that the more contemporary theorizing of the left needs to be situated. However, before proceeding to discuss those more contemporary developments it will be of value to reflect on the competing criminological perspectives addressed here.

Conclusion

Obviously it is very difficult in one chapter to do justice to the range of ideas which have been touched upon here. What is significant for this book, however, is to consider the extent to which the ideas which have been discussed here still have some relevance for the criminological agenda. A recurring theme in this respect is the whole question of the relative importance to be attached to social factors and individual factors in constructing a theory or an explanation of crime. This tension remains. As the following chapters unfold the continuing importance of this tension will become increasingly apparent.

In addition it is useful to reflect upon what has remained unspoken in these competing perspectives. Indeed, until the later developments within critical criminology, questions of race and gender are barely articulated in the criminological world. Addressing these issues is certainly much more upfront in current criminological concerns than these perspectives would suggest. The whole question of gendering criminology is discussed in Chapter 5.

However what clearly remains present within these and subsequent criminological theories is the attachment to the modernist project. The desire to work towards the effective implementation of change, whether that be micro policy changes or macro societal change, is deeply embedded in the criminological agenda. The extent to which that continues both to manifest itself and to limit the criminological world view will be returned to in the chapters which follow.

Further reading

A range of general introductions to criminological theory are now available and will offer a more detailed appreciation of the competing perspectives around than can be discussed here. See, for example, Gibbons (1994) *Talking about Crime and Criminals* or Williams and McShane (1994) *Criminological Theory*. A particularly interesting approach is offered by Lilly, Cullen and Ball (1995) *Criminological Theory: Context and Consequences*. This book locates the different theories it discusses in the different social and political contexts in which they emerged which makes for interesting reading. Finally, there is no doubt that reading *The New Criminology* (1973) by Taylor, Walton and Young is a must for anyone seriously wanting to appreciate the unfolding nature of criminological theory.

chapter three

Understanding 'right realism'

Viewed from the 1990s it is easy to observe that 1979 marked a major shift in political and economic debate in the UK as Chapter 1 has suggested. The underlying cause of this shift was the changing world economic climate of the 1970s. That process resulted in governments, both in the UK and else-where, targeting cuts in public expenditure as one way of managing the impact of such a worldwide recession. This underlying imperative brought the delivery of public services into the spotlight in a way which had not been experienced before, especially in the UK; this imperative consequently altered, fundamentally, the way in which social problems and proposed solutions to social problems were debated. It is important to appreciate the nature of this change in order to understand the emergence and influence of ideas referred to as 'right realism'.

The commitment to the welfare ethic of the 1950s reflected an underlying belief that social problems could be solved socially, that is through the pro-vision of adequate social and economic conditions. If such conditions were provided then social problems, including the problem of crime, would dis-appear. The continuing rising crime rate alongside worldwide recession, how-ever, called a halt to this way of addressing social problems and paved the way for a different way of thinking and talking about crime and the crime problem. That different way of thinking was characterized primarily by a re-emergence of a focus on the the cause of crime lying within individual processes rather than social ones. Centring the individual, and the notion of individual responsibility, in this way became embedded in a whole range of political and policy imperatives, including crime, associated with the Conservative Party of the 1980s. This focus provided the general climate in which varieties of 'right realist' thinking became more prominent at this particular historical moment.

The shift to the right politically in the UK was paralleled by similar developments in the United States. It was there where, arguably, the emergence of a range of criminological ideas which might be loosely labelled 'right realism' first emerged. While such ideas are largely associated with American writers, they resonated politically with some aspects of the law and order debate which ensued in the UK. The concern of this chapter, therefore, will be to try to untangle the political and intellectual connections which can be made between criminological right realism and such changes in direction in criminal justice policy.

It is also important to note that, as Young (1994) points out, criminological theories have both an interior and an exterior history. In other words, it is as valuable to appreciate the social and political context which deems theories relevant as it is to understand the intricacies of the theories themselves. Significantly, what underpins the more current theoretical concerns to be discussed here is a long standing tension between the relative importance to be attached to the social as against the biological in constructing an explanation of crime as discussed in Chapter 2. This tension and the wider political context in which this tension re-emerged are the two factors which inform the concerns of this and the following chapter in which varieties of realism of the 1980s are discussed.

So what kind of theoretical work might be considered to constitute 'right realism'? Here we shall discuss four different theoretical and/or policy strands under this heading: socio-biological explanations, rational choice theory, the routine activity approach, and that which has been called administrative criminology.

Socio-biological explanations: the work of Wilson and Herrnstein

Young (1994) observes that James Q. Wilson is an enormously influential figure in American criminology. Moreover, given the much higher crime rate of the United States, especially with respect to levels of violence, such conservatively oriented thinking as that which is found in the work of Wilson also has a high political and policy profile. While his book *Thinking about Crime* (1975) considerably influenced political and policy thinking, his work with Richard Herrnstein *Crime and Human Nature* (Wilson and Herrnstein, 1985) offers a more definitive theoretical account of what, in their view, constitute the underlying causes of crime. This account has three elements:

constitutional factors, the presence and/or absence of reinforcers, and the nature of conscience. Each of these will be discussed in turn.

Crime is an activity disproportionately carried out by young men living in large cities. There are old criminals, and female ones, and rural and small town ones, but to a much greater degree than would be expected by chance, criminals are young urban males.

(Wilson and Herrnstein, 1985: 26)

The foregoing statement can be read in a number of different ways. In one sense it can be argued that it articulates a very clear understanding of what constitutes the central problem for all those in the criminal justice industry: the highly problematic nature of the behaviour of young (urban) males. As such it could be said that it resonates very well with the work of those concerned to 'gender' criminology (see Chapter 5).

However, while those concerned to gender criminology problematize the issue of young men in relation to the expression of their masculinity as a socially constructed process, Wilson and Herrnstein proceed to explain the behaviour of young men by reference to them being just that – young men. In other words, they prefer to foreground in their explanation of the differences between the criminal behaviour of the sexes what they call constitutional factors. Such factors are not necessarily genetic but certainly have some biological origin. So, as Wilson and Herrnstein state:

It is likely that the effect of maleness and youthfulness on the tendency to commit crime has both constitutional and social origins: that is, it has something to do with the biological status of being a young male and with how that young man has been treated by family, friends and society.

(Wilson and Herrnstein, 1985: 69)

So, as we shall see, their explanation is not solely rooted in biology, but reflects a concern to construct an explanation of criminal behaviour in which factors, such as sex, age, intelligence, body type and personality, are inserted as potential biological givens (though not necessarily determiners of action) of human beings projected into a social world – a social world in which the individual learns what kind of behaviour is rewarded under what circumstances. This is the second element of their theory.

Drawing implicitly on the work of psychologist B. F. Skinner, Wilson and Herrnstein place themselves squarely within psychological behaviourism. Put simply, this theory puts forward the view that individuals learn to respond to situations in accordance with how their behaviour has been rewarded and punished on previous occasions. According to the Skinnerian approach, the environment can operate (hence the term 'operant conditioning') to produce the kind of behavioural response most wanted from an individual. In order to understand the propensity to commit crime, therefore, it is important to understand the ways in which the environment might operate upon individuals, whose constitutional make-up might be different, to produce this response. Within this general learning framework, then, Wilson and Herrnstein locate the influence of the family, the school, and the wider community.

This general learning environment is always very carefully explored by these authors so that sight is never lost of the important influence that individual differences can have on the learning process. So while certain family backgrounds might potentially spell trouble in relation to crime, that is not always the determined outcome. The constitutional factors mentioned above might serve to make a difference as might the power of the third element to their theory: the conscience.

In this last respect Wilson and Herrnstein support the statement made by Eysenck that 'conscience is a conditioned reflex' (1985: 125). In this sense they are asserting that some people during childhood have so effectively internalized law abiding behaviour that they would never be tempted to behave otherwise. For others, breaking the law might be dependent upon the particular circumstances of a particular situation suggesting less effective internalization of such rules. For yet others, the failure to appreciate the likely consequences of their actions might lead them into criminal behaviour under any circumstances. In other words, the effectiveness of something that is called 'the conscience' may co-vary with the individual's constitution and the learning environment in which people find themselves.

These three elements then – constitutional factors, the presence and/or absence of positive and negative behavioural reinforcers alongside the strength of the conscience – provide the framework in which Wilson and Herrnstein offer an explanation of crime. For them the interplay between these factors can explain why crime rates may increase both in times of prosperity and of recession since the equation between the social and the individual is a complex one. Hence they suggest,

> Long term trends in crime rates can be accounted for primarily by three factors. First shifts in the age structure of the population will increase or decrease the proportion of persons – young males – in the population who are likely to be temperamentally aggressive and to have short time horizons. Second changes in the benefits of crime . . . and in the cost of crime . . . will change the rate at which crimes occur, especially property crimes . . . Third, broad social and cultural changes in the level and intensity of society's investment (via families, schools, churches, and the mass media) in inculcating an internalized commitment to self control will affect the extent to which individuals at risk are willing to postpone gratification, accept as equitable the outcomes of others, and conform to rules.
>
> (Wilson and Herrnstein, 1985: 437)

Given the complex interplay of these factors, and given the variables which these authors wish to highlight as constituting the key underpinning causes of crime, it might be possible to conclude that such a framework merely adds, in a fundamental way, to the view that nothing can be done about crime. This is not the conclusion reached by Wilson and Herrnstein. Their view is that while not enough may be known about what works under what conditions, marginal gains can be made by targeting what is known. This might take the form of, for example, tougher sentences for repeat offenders, and/or working in a concentrated way in high crime areas still deemed to be rescuable, or any combination of policies like these, so long as such policies are focused and 'doable'.

In this respect, as Young (1994) argues, their concern is primarily with maintaining social order rather than necessarily delivering justice and their focus is with what can be done rather than with trying to achieve Utopia. However, their theory also marks a revitalization of ideas which some criminologists would regard as more than unfortunate, especially the sympathetic way in which constitutional factors are dealt with.

However, it is equally the case that a broad based concern with the potential contribution of biological factors never really disappeared from the criminological agenda. That such factors were given greater prominence during the 1980s is, arguably, a product of the cultural and economic heightening of possessive individualism. This has been more colloquially expressed as the emergence of the 'me generation', in which the individual, and individual success, became the centre of all kinds of activities, including crime. It is no surprise, then, that within the heightening of these processes, a view focusing on the individual and individual potentialities should become popular. Those same circumstances have also proved to be the context in which a view of the individual criminal as an economic decision maker also became increasingly attractive. Such a view underpins the second variety of 'right realism' to be discussed here: rational choice theory.

Rational choice theory

Rational choice theory, alongside the routine activity approach to be discussed below, are visions of the crime problem which have informed what Young (1986) labelled 'administrative criminology'. This version of criminology was largely associated with work emanating from the Home Office in the UK during the early 1980s and will be discussed in greater detail shortly. It will be of value to develop an overall appreciation of rational choice theory first of all.

Gibbons (1994) argues that rational choice theory neither constitutes a new nor a general explanation of crime since elements of attributing the ability to make choices and decisions to criminals and criminal behaviour are present in a range of criminological perspectives. However, in contrast with earlier concerns with the rationality or otherwise of the offender, the concerns of rational choice theory are framed to address the central question of crime prevention. It is in this respect especially that Young (1994) argues that rational choice theory (in its embodiment within administrative criminology) refuses to address the causes of crime but is more concerned with its management. Indeed, in support of this view, Clarke (1980), one of the main proponents of this version of criminology, accuses earlier criminological perspectives as suffering from 'predispositional bias'. Thus he states:

> criminological theories have been little concerned with the situational determinants of crime. Instead, the main object of these theories (whether biological, psychological, or sociological in orientation) has been to show how some people are born with, or come to acquire a 'disposition' to behave in a consistently criminal manner.
>
> (Clarke, 1980: 137)

This bias, he goes on to argue, has had unfortunate consequences for the issue of crime prevention:

> These difficulties are primarily practical, but they also reflect the uncertainties and inconsistencies of treating distant psychological events and social processes as the 'causes' of crime. Given that each event is in turn caused by others, at what point in the infinitely regressive chain should one stop in the search for effective points of intervention?
>
> (Clarke, 1980: 138)

For Clarke (and later Cornish and Clarke, 1986), effective intervention can be established by understanding the criminal as an economic decision maker.

The idea of treating human beings as driven by the motive of profit maximization is one which has a longstanding tradition within the discipline of economics. This idea presumes that individuals make rational decisions on the basis of the costs and benefits that alternative courses of action have for them:

> offenders seek to benefit themselves by their criminal behaviour; that this involves the making of decisions and choices, however rudimentary on occasion these processes might be; and that these processes exhibit a measure of rationality, albeit constrained by the limits of time and the availability of information.
>
> (Cornish and Clarke, 1986: 1)

This rational process of decision making is used to account for not only the decision to commit crime but also the time and the place in which such crime is committed. However, some effort is made to recognize that such decision making may be limited by the availability of information or inaccurate information. So, as can be seen, the rational choice model of criminology, while influenced by the assumed rationality of the economic human being, contains within it an appreciation that such rationality is limited.

The value of this perspective, as was suggested earlier, has been argued for within the context of its crime prevention potential, usually referred to as situational crime prevention. As Gibbons states:

> If many offenders, and predatory offenders in particular, weigh at least some of the potential risks against the gains they anticipate from law-breaking, criminal acts may often be deterred by making them riskier or harder to carry out.
>
> (Gibbons, 1994: 125)

By implication, then, the harder the target of criminal behaviour, the more likely the criminal will choose another target. This, of course, illuminates the central problem of the rational choice model formulated in this way; displacement, what happens to the motive for profit maximization once the decision to commit crime has been made, is this transformed into something else?

Of course, since the rational choice model is not centrally concerned to address the underlying causes of crime, the question posed above is of little consequence. It is a question, however, which is not easily sidestepped given the practical implications of this way of thinking about crime. Every crime prevention policy carries with it some costs whether those costs be quantitative (i.e. resource led) or qualitative (i.e. social), and these need to be weighed against the potential gains of the kinds of situational measures that Clarke and Cornish propose.

In any event this way of thinking about crime has been very influential in reorienting crime prevention policy towards victimization prevention policy (Karmen, 1990). In addition it has served to fuel political debate about the crime problem by focusing attention on preventing the behaviour of the individual criminal at a time when alternative policy initiatives might be considerably more expensive.

Of course, crime does not only occur because there is an offender so motivated to commit crime. What rational choice theory also presumes is that there must be the opportunity for crime to be committed. The next approach to be considered as a variety of right realism, the routine activity approach, takes the appreciation of this relationship between the offender and the opportunity to commit crime a stage further.

The routine activity approach

This version of 'right realism' takes our thinking about crime beyond the individual *per se* and endeavours to locate that individual behaviour in a wider social context. It has its origins in the work of Cohen and Felson

(1979) and argues that crime is the product of three factors coming together in particular times and places: a motivated offender, a potential victim, and the absence of a capable guardian. These three factors can be identified in people's daily, routine behaviours and their patterning may alter the times and places in which crime occurs but their conjunction provides the framework within which crime takes place.

Routine activity theory does not purport to explain the motivation for crime nor does it offer an explanation of the broader social framework which may facilitate some patterns between these three variables as opposed to others. Moreover it does little to explain why some guardians might prove to be more capable than others. Neither does it endeavour to say much about why it is that some individual behaviours render them more susceptible to victimization than others. However, as a theory it does recognize that there is a systematic patterning to crime, redolent of the social ecology approach discussed in Chapter 2.

In this sense, it is an approach which has generated empirical findings which have been used to support a largely conservative orientation to criminal justice policy. Indeed, its limited conceptualization of the social does allow for the possibility of including variables, other than just the individual offender, into the criminological equation. This has been especially the case with respect to understanding the nature and extent of criminal victimization. It is primarily in this latter respect that the influence of the routine activity approach can be found within 'administrative criminology'. This influence has been felt most through the concept of lifestyle.

The connections between 'administrative' criminology and routine activity approach are to be found in the influence of the work of Hindelang, Gottfredson, and Garofalo (1978). The parallels between these ideas and those of Cohen and Felson have been discussed by Garofalo (1986). Focusing more on the routine activity elements to the question of lifestyle, they state that for personal victimization to occur:

First the prime actors – the offender and the victim – must have occasion to intersect in time and space. Second some source of dispute or claim must arise between the actors in which the victim is perceived by the offender as an appropriate object of victimization. Third, the offender must be willing and able to threaten or use force (or stealth) in order to achieve the desired end. Fourth, the circumstances must be such that the offender views it as advantageous to use or threaten force (or stealth) to achieve the desired end. The probability of these conditions being met is related to the life circumstances of members of society.

(Hindelang *et al.*, 1978: 250)

These authors go on to offer eight propositions designed to cast light on why some individuals are much more likely to be subject to personal victimization than others as a result of variations in exposure to different levels of risk reflected in their lifestyle.

These propositions, then, draw attention to the importance of variables such as age, sex and race but also address the different routine patterns of behaviour which potentially expose people of different ages, races and sex to different levels of victimization. These patterns would include the amount of time spent in public places, how often people use public transport, and at what time of day people find themselves in such circumstances. Of course, in all of these circumstances there may be an appropriate guardian absent or present. This will feed into overall levels of victimization, as Cohen and Felson's schema suggests.

A detailed critique of the work of Hindelang *et al.* (1978) can be found in Walklate (1989). The value of this way of thinking about crime in this context is the particular relevance it has in understanding the final variation in 'right realism' to be discussed here – the administrative criminology of the Home Office.

Administrative criminology

In some respects it is dubious as to whether or not such a criminology, as a coherent set of propositions, exists, and/or whether indeed it counts as a variety of 'right realism' in the same sense that the work of Wilson and Herrnstein can be so identified. However, since this label for the work emanating from the Home Office was first coined, it has gained some considerable currency, and for the purposes of clarity it has been adopted here. First of all, it will be useful to summarize what Young (1994) has characterized as administrative criminology since it is his label which has had such a powerful impact.

Young (1986) squarely locates the emergence of administrative criminology as following from the failure of what he calls 'social democratic positivism'. That position, both academically and politically, had endeavoured to centre the idea that crime was caused by social conditions and what was necessary to combat crime was to change those conditions. Yet despite efforts to change those social conditions the crime rate still rose. And while some might have argued that such a rise in crime rate was no more (and no less) than an artefact of changing policing practices, administrative criminology at least took seriously the problematic nature of the rising crime rate. This is the clear point of convergence between this work and the other versions of right realism discussed here.

However, administrative criminology, as suggested earlier, sidesteps the question of what the underpinning cause of that rising crime rate might be. In Young's words, it fails to address the aetiological crisis within criminology. Another similarity with other versions of 'right realism' discussed here (perhaps in fairness with the exception of Wilson and Herrnstein). As a result of sidestepping this issue, the work emanating from the Home Office during the 1980s was characterized as 'administrative' in so far as its central concern became administering , that is managing the crime problem, rather than working to explore its underlying causes.

Young (1994) identifies the main theoretical input of this work as being rational choice theory. Indeed, Clarke, a proponent of rational choice theory as discussed earlier, was a central figure in the Home Office during the early 1980s. However, if the underlying presumptions of the British Crime Survey are explored a little more carefully it is also possible to see that routine activity theory, particularly through the concept of lifestyle, had its part to play in the formulation and the subsequent dissemination of these survey findings.

The British Crime Survey has been a vital source of political and policy information since the first survey was conducted in 1982. Conducted at regular intervals since then, the British Crime Survey has provided a very valuable database for both estimating the 'dark' figure of crime and for informing the policy making process. Its questions, especially in relation to the patterning of criminal victimization, very much reflect the routine activity lifestyle concerns of Hindelang and others. In this respect it has been possible to construct images of who is most likely to be personally criminally victimized which challenge conventional media images; the young male who uses public transport and goes out drinking two or three times a week as opposed to the elderly housebound female, for example. However, the findings of the British Crime Survey have not only been used to challenge media images of victimization. They have also been used more or less explicitly for political purposes. It is perhaps in this latter respect that the work emanating from the Home Office is best described as a version of 'right realism'.

Mayhew and Hough (1988) describe the initial thinking behind the formulation of the first British Crime Survey in the following way:

> It was thought within the Home Office that distorted and exaggerated ideas of crime levels, trends and risks were widespread among the public, information on crime risks would demonstrate the comparatively low risks of serious crime, and puncture inacccurate stereotypes of crime victims. In other words, the survey was envisaged in part at least as a way of achieving what might be called the 'normalisation' of crime – to help create a less alarmist and more balanced climate of opinion about law and order.
>
> (Mayhew and Hough, 1988: 157)

That more balanced climate of opinion was intended to address not only what were perceived to be the exaggerated fears of the public about crime, but also the question of resourcing law and order issues. Thus that same database could be used, and has been used, to bolster the campaign for the development and refinement of crime prevention initiatives (in the fashion of situational crime prevention) rather than necessarily finding funds for more police officers. This strategy was clearly adopted in the mid-1980s with a commitment and a vigour not previously experienced before by the police as a public institution.

In this sense, then, this kind of criminological work clearly lent support to a government committed to cuts in public expenditure via the mechanisms of demanding 'value for money' and 'efficiency' in a general political and economic climate working to recast the citizen as a consumer of public services – a consumer of public services in a social context in which there was 'no such thing as society'. This last comment and its implied denial of the importance of underlying social structures, famously made by the then Prime Minister Margaret Thatcher in the mid-1980s, leads us to a more careful consideration of what is both 'right' and 'real' about 'right realism'.

Right realism: a critique

As Lilly, Cullen and Ball (1995) argue, there is no necessary connection between the theories discussed here and the adoption of conservative policy implications. However, the focus on the individual which is embedded in all these theories lends itself most readily to such an interpretation in particular social contexts. So it is clear to see how, at times of economic stringency, there might be an easy match to be made between holding the individual, or individual deficiencies, responsible for social problems and the drive to cutback public expenditure. This view, of course, contains within it an inconsistency (as we shall see below) but focusing on that which goes on within the individual, presumes that society and all its inequities is given and nonproblematic (there is such a thing as society!). Thus this kind of criminology can avoid considering the potential interrelationship between individual 'deficiencies' and social 'deficiencies'.

In commenting on Wilson and Herrnstein's work, for example, Lilly, Cullen and Ball have this to say:

> Wilson and Herrnstein's work implied that certain biological dispositions, found frequently in the poor, may be responsible for excessive criminal behaviour . . . The historical record teaches that attempts to root crime in human nature exempt the social fabric from blame and lend credence to the idea that offenders are largely beyond reform and in need of punitive control.
>
> (Lilly *et al.*, 1995: 215)

These ideological implications result regardless of how carefully the authors themselves may frame their argument.

The resurgence of the idea that offenders are largely wicked or beyond control, of course, results in policy inconsistencies, if not contradictions. On the one hand, the economic and political conditions which render such ideas popular demand a withdrawal of the state. On the other hand, the policy initiatives which flow from taking these ideas seriously imply deterrence from criminality in the form of incapacitation of various kinds, which by implication also requires the greater involvement of the state as an overseer and/or deliverer of incapacitation. The extent to which successive Home Secretaries have campaigned for tougher prison sentences as an answer to the crime problem stands as testimony to this. Yet this is also the most expensive form of state intervention possible within the criminal justice arena which at the same time has little empirical support as being an effective measure against the crime problem. A conservative would argue, however, that it is more than effective against particular criminals since it keeps them out of circulation; as Wilson (1975: 235) explains, 'Wicked people exist. Nothing avails except to set them apart from innocent people.' So this perhaps demonstrates what is 'right' about right realism; but what is 'real' about it?

The question of what is 'real' about right realism raises a similar dilemma as there is with 'left realism'. Put relatively simply at this juncture, the use of the term realism in this context is more political than it is philosophical. In this sense, one feature which binds these different theoretical perspectives together, is that they all take the rising crime rate as a real problem to be tackled. In other words, the crime rate is not to be seen simply as a product of either changes in reporting behaviour, or changes in the recording practices of criminal justice officials, or a product of changes in implementation of the law. It is to be seen as a real indicator of a real social problem. It is in this sense that right realism and left realism share a common starting point.

This usage of the term realism is, however, political – political in the sense that it is used to claim the territory of crime and criminal justice policy as a real issue to be addressed by the political domain. A philosophical use of the term realism would be much more concerned to identify the underlying causes (or as Bhaskar (1978) would say, the generative mechanisms) which serve to produce the surface manifestation of, in this case, an increasing crime rate. This use of the term realism arguably locates any analysis of a social problem within the realm of the social rather than the individual. As we have seen the theories discussed here resist such an interpretation.

To summarize: while there are varieties within what might be called 'right realism' the common ground between these variations lies in their commitment to accepting that crime is a real problem and in their focus on understanding the individual and the role of individual differences as the key to tackling that crime problem. These common concerns render their policy focus as being one primarily concerned with the maintenance of social order. The politically conservative implications of this work are clearly evident.

Given these common concerns it is also clearly understandable that the conservative policy implications of these theories have been pursued with greater vigour in a time of more right wing politics and economics than the more liberal implications which might follow from the work discussed here. The recognition of this intertwining of the political and academic highlights a further source of criticism for this kind of criminology.

As was observed in Chapter 1, the emergence of criminology as a discipline was intimately connected with the policy making process: the desire to manage social change. In this sense, criminology, it has been argued, is intimately connected to the modernist project. This interconnection is clearly demonstrated in the work of the right realists and the use to which their ideas have been put in the policy arena. Crime in this context is used both to signify a social problem and to unify support for dealing with that problem. Assumptions such as these are challenged by the work of the postmodernists. They would argue that the presumption of such unity is highly problematic given the increasing importance attached to difference and diversity in the (post)modern world. Recognition of difference and diversity, therefore renders the traditional relationship between criminology and the policy making process a highly problematic, if not a dubious, one. From this point of view right realism makes little sense at all. These issues are returned to in Chapter 4.

Conclusion

Lilly, Cullen and Ball (1995) point out that

> The 1980s saw a return to ways of thinking about crime that although packaged in different language, revitalized the old idea that the sources of lawlessness reside in individuals, not within the social fabric. The rekindling of this type of theorising, we believe, was no coincidence. Like other theories before it, conservative theory drew its power and popularity from the prevailing social context.
>
> (Lilly *et al.*, 1995: 223)

Both this chapter, and the one which follows, lay bare the political interconnections between criminology and criminal justice policy. These interconnections have become more transparent, arguably, as the needs of the (capitalist) state have become more demanding. The underlying drive of 'possessive individualism', whether articulated in the Marxian sense or in the more liberal tones of the work of Daniel Bell (1976), celebrate the power of the individual in both positive and negative ways. In this sense there is perhaps little to argue with some aspects of Wilson's arguments in which he asserts that crime and a rising crime rate are the price to be paid for (American) capitalism. There is, however, no necessary corollary between this assertion and the drive towards incapacitation as a way of solving the problem, though it does point to the view that it is highly unlikely that such processes can be reversed. It is out of recognition of the reality of this, and the increasingly powerful influence of right realism thinking that left realism was borne.

Young (1994) argues that there are four points of convergence between right realism and left realism. It is worth quoting Young at length on this:

1. Both see crime as really being a problem; both see the public's fear of crime as having a rational basis, in contrast to left idealism and administrative criminology.
2. Both believe that the reality of crime control has been misconceived, particularly the centrality of the public–police relationship.
3. Both are realistic about what can be done about crime and the limitations of our present-day knowledge. Neither disdains marginal gains, whilst both discount utopian solutions.
4. Both emphasize the need for closely monitored research and intervention and are critical of the widespread tendency to 'throw money' at the crime problem without attempting to measure cost-effectiveness.

(Young, 1994: 102)

The extent to which these points of convergence are more apparent than real will become more evident in Chapter 4, in which 'left realism' will be discussed in detail.

To summarize: the emergence of 'right realism' within criminology was a result of what was perceived to be the failure of more liberal stances on criminal justice process, a view which in and of itself was also clearly connected to changing social and economic circumstances. Out of these circumstances, it is no great surprise that in some respects a resurgence of interest in the more classical criminological ideas (discussed in Chapter 2) should occur. Certainly a focus on the individual absolves governments of responsibility on the one hand and expects greater responsibility of individual citizens on the other. The changing nature of this relationship between the citizen and the state will be a recurring theme throughout this book but especially in Chapters 6 and 7.

Further reading

As this chapter has demonstrated, there is no easily identifiable body of knowledge called 'right realism'. However, those interested in pursuing this line of thinking could do worse than to read Wilson and Herrnstein (1985) *Crime and Human Nature*. It can certainly pay to read material in its original form and this book provides a very sound empirical and theoretical basis from which the term 'right realism' has been constructed. An explication of rational choice theory and its relevance to criminology is best found in Cornish and Clarke (1986) *The Reasoning Criminal: Rational Choice Perspectives on Offending.*

Understanding 'left realism'

One way of appreciating the relevance of any social theory is to locate the emergence and development of that theory in its political and social context. The 'left realist' approach to criminology is no exception to this general rule. While some have endeavoured to identify traces of 'left realist' ideas to the mid-1970s (Lowman, 1992), political and social events in the UK of the late 1970s and early 1980s substantially aided the development of these ideas. In particular, the election of the Conservative Party to office on a strong law and order ticket under the leadership of Margaret Thatcher in 1979, the civil disturbances in a number of inner city areas in 1981, and the re-election of Margaret Thatcher in 1983, constituted some of the events which proved to sharpen the political and academic debate on the crime problem. Chapter 3 has already indicated the presence and influence of a 'conservative criminology' promoted under the auspices of 'right realism' which was, arguably, informing some Home Office policy thinking during this time. So it is against this general background of social, policy, and political events that the term 'radical left realism', later to be referred to as simply 'left realism', was coined by Young, to connote an alternative way of talking about the crime problem to that offered by the general conservatism of the early 1980s.

Arguably, it is not until 1985 onwards (Matthews and Young, 1992), in the aftermath of the Merseyside and Islington Crime Surveys formulated and conducted under the umbrella of 'left realism', that this theoretical position really emerged as espousing a relatively coherent set of ideas with a concomitant policy agenda. Since that time there has been both a consolidation and critique of these ideas. Their presence and influence has extended beyond the UK as they have been modified and applied in different international contexts.

This chapter will endeavour to analyse and trace the development of these ideas since 1979. In so doing particular attention will be paid first of all to the conceptual development of the central 'left realist' ideas found primarily in the work of Lea, Matthews and Young. Second, these ideas will be compared and contrasted with other versions of 'left realism', paying especial attention to the work of Elliott Currie. Third, we shall examine the methodological and policy agendas which flow from 'left realism'. Fourth, an overview of the various critiques of these ideas will be offered, followed by a special reference to the relationship between 'left realism' and feminism. Finally, we shall consider the relative merits and achievements of this strand of criminological work. But first, what is left realism?

What is 'left realism'?

The central tenet of left realism is to reflect the reality of crime, that is in its origins, its nature and its impact. This involves a rejection of the tendencies to romanticize crime or to pathologize it, to analyze solely from the point of view of the administration of crime or the criminal actor, to understand crime or to exaggerate it. And our understanding of methodology, our interpretation of the statistics, our notions of aetiology follow from this. Most importantly, it is realism which informs our notion of practice: in answering what can be done about the problems of crime and social control.

(Young, 1986: 21)

This desire to reflect the reality of crime and the crime experience, for Young, distinguishes 'left realism' from what he has labelled 'left idealism' as well as from the administrative criminology of the Home Office. In his view 'left idealism' neglected the problem of the cause of crime. In 'left idealism' the cause of crime is constituted as either an artefact of the state's need to criminalize in order to sustain itself as a consequence of the crisis of capitalism, or the cause of crime is so obvious that it requires no further explanation (the notion that poverty obviously causes crime, for example). On the one hand the first assertion reflects a remarkably simplistic view of the state, how it operates, and the relationship between individual citizens and the state. On the other hand, the second assertion assumes a rational economic view of human action which fails, at a minimum, to resonate with the empirical evidence.

In addition, Young argued that administrative criminology also side-stepped the problem of the cause of crime; for the administrativist the key criminological problem is how to manage the crime problem, not how to explain it. This lack of concern with aetiology (causes), for Young renders both of these positions similar in so far as they reflect a concern with the mechanisms and management of the social control and/or social construction of crime rather than a concern with the potentially much more complex processes which feed into and generate the 'crime problem'.

So, in part the 'left realist' agenda emerged as a reaction to dissatisfaction with the (then) state of criminological theorizing. However, 'left realism' set itself up, not just reactively but also proactively, as a way of thinking about the contemporary reality of the crime problem which pointed to an increasing awareness of the nature and extent of criminal victimization. Indeed, it was the Home Office sponsored 'administrative' research in the form of the development of the criminal victimization survey which contributed to the need for greater awareness of, and sensitivity to, the complex ways in which crime impacts upon both individuals and communities. It is the complexity of these processes which left realism claims to address.

Left realism starts from a position which centralizes the need to address 'problems as people experience them' (Young, 1986: 24). It 'necessitates an accurate victimology' (ibid.: 23), it 'must (also) trace accurately the relationship between victim and offender' (ibid.) and must note that 'crime is focused both geographically and socially on the most vulnerable sections of the community' (ibid.). These concerns form the fundamental basis to the realist position echoing what was later called a focus on the 'square of crime' (J. Young, 1992: 27). So

> The most fundamental tenet of realism is that criminology should be faithful to the nature of crime. That is, it should acknowledge the form of crime, the social context of crime, the shape of crime, its trajectory through time, and its enactment in space.
>
> (J. Young, 1992: 26)

This tenet provides for four elements to understanding crime (hence the 'square of crime'); the victim, the offender, the reaction of the formal agencies of the state, and the reaction of the public. Thus, for example, the crime rate needs to be understood as a product of the interaction of all these four points; changes in the offending population, changes in the victim population, policy changes within the formal agencies, and changes in the reactions of the public to different kinds of crimes. All of which may, of course, vary independently of each other and may differ for different crimes (what

Young refers to as understanding the 'shape of crime'). Thus any explanation of crime needs to be fourfold in character; in other words, it makes little sense to privilege an explanation which centres police activity, for example, over that of criminal activity. What, then, is the key explanatory concept employed by 'left realism'?

The key explanatory concept employed by 'left realism' is that of 'relative deprivation'. This concept has a substantial history in both sociology and social psychology, and denotes understanding the conditions in which people not only may be (or indeed may not at all be) objectively deprived, but also may feel so deprived and may perceive themselves to be so deprived in comparison with either others in the same social category or others in a different social category. As a cause of crime Jock Young (1992) argues that relative deprivation is very powerful for three reasons; it can apply to circumstances throughout the social structure, it can be applied to all kinds of crime not just those which may be deemed economically motivated, and it is a concept which is not dependent on identifying some absolute standard of deprivation or poverty. Utilizing the concept of relative deprivation in this way is not intended to suggest that there is one causal explanation for crime, but serves as a conceptual framework for understanding the social circumstances in which crime is likely to occur. In other words, it is important, left realists argue, to understand the ways in which the experience of relative deprivation may be differently constituted under different circumstances: the principle of specificity.

Jock Young (1992) argues that there are three major problems associated with the question of specificity which have both underpinned and undermined criminological thinking; a presumption that understanding male working-class crime equates with understanding all criminal behaviour, a presumption that understanding crime in advanced industrial societies equates with an understanding of crime in general, and a presumption that American criminological theorizing (produced in a very atypical society in terms of criminal behaviour) provides theorizing which is applicable elsewhere. In other words, while the concept of relative deprivation might be powerful, what it reveals about social and personal processes in one society needs to be quite tightly articulated and differentiated, that is specified, from what might be revealed through its application in a different social context. For 'left realism' understanding the specific circumstances in which crime occurs can be achieved through the 'principle of lived realities'.

Focusing on 'lived realities' implies two concerns. The first addresses the potentially complex ways in which key socio-structural variables may interact with each other to produce differential experiences of crime. So, for example, there is evidence to suggest that the differential experience of young white males being stopped by the police, as compared with young black males, is lessened when social class is controlled for. Appreciating the complex ways in which variables interact with each other implies, of course, that simply to assert the importance of one variable over another might result in the distortion of not only the empirical data but also the reality of people's everyday experiences. The second concern foregrounds the need to place behaviour in its social context, whether that be criminal behaviour or police behaviour. It is important, for example, to appreciate that police behaviour is not merely the product of a 'macho cop culture' but the end result of understanding the specific nature of the task in hand alongside the strategy chosen to deal with that task.

'Realism, then, does not deal in abstractions: the principle of specificity demands that explanation be grounded' (J. Young, 1992: 40). In other words, there may be different underlying causal and motivational factors contributing to different types of crime in different types of settings. An appreciation of which may require different kinds of responses from the agencies of social control. This takes us to the next principle of left realism: how crime might be controlled and the role of the social control agencies in that process.

'The control of crime must reflect the nature of crime' (J. Young, 1992: 41). This has a number of implications. First, it involves activity at each point in the square of crime. That is the control of crime requires a response from both the formal and the informal agencies of social control for both the victim and the offender. Second, the control of crime involves appreciating that crime occurs in both a spatial and temporal setting, both of which are considerations which need to be built into crime prevention policy. Third, while realism favours structural intervention to prevent crime this does not preclude proceeding with a whole range of different crime prevention strategies provided that they are put in place in settings and circumstances in which they have been shown to have some demonstrable effect. Fourth, while realists favour the retention of criminal justice sanctions for some crimes, crime control for the left realist involves recognizing that the process of criminalization is politically informed and that it is both possible and desirable to find means through which that process can be more widely and effectively democratized.

Recognizing that some crimes are more difficult to control than others and recognizing that a much more careful consideration and debate around the role of the police in the crime control process needs to be made, Jock Young states that:

> It is not the 'Thin Blue Line', but the social bricks and mortar of civil society which are the major bulwarks against crime. Good jobs with a discernible future, housing estates that tenants can be proud of, community facilities which enhance a sense of cohesion and belonging, a reduction in unfair inequalities, all create a society which is more cohesive and less criminogenic.
>
> (J. Young, 1992: 45)

If this is the case it is both misplaced and foolish to overemphasize both the role of the police in contributing to the process of criminalization and to crime control. What is necessary is a concerted and coordinated response by all those agencies who potentially may have an impact on crime: the principle of multi-agency intervention.

Left realism argues that it is only through multi-agency intervention that the reality of crime can be tackled. This is because of the variable nature of crime itself and the multifaceted nature of social control. A commitment to the principle of multi-agency intervention does not imply a blanket application of that principle. Different crimes may require the cooperation of different agencies at different points in the commission of that crime for both the victim and the offender. They may require the formation of different types of relationships between the relevant agencies, and may require different levels of participation with and from the public. Much of the work to date around multi-agency intervention has neglected to pay attention to the complex processes which may inhibit or facilitate such working, under what conditions, and with what kind of support from the public. For left realism such initiatives need to be much more carefully and finely tuned to the reality of crime in order for them to work.

An effective relationship with the public is seen to be one of the elements of multi-agency intervention which can facilitate or hinder its working. Indeed the public have a crucial role to play in formulating a policy response to the crime problem. This alludes to the next principle of left realism: the principle of rational democratic input. Democratic input recognizes the need to take people seriously. At one level this is economic; the public pay for public safety so in that sense they have a right to be consulted in how that public safety is constructed. At another level it is also important to recognize that the public also have a range of worries and concerns about their safety. In this sense there is a voice here to be heard in the way in which such worries may, or may not be alleviated. Such democratic input is to be achieved through the social survey.

> The social survey is a democratic instrument: it provides a reasonably accurate appraisal of people's fears and of their experience of victimization . . . Social surveys, therefore, allow us to give voice to the experience of people, and they enable us to differentiate the safety needs of different sectors of the community.
>
> (J. Young, 1992: 50)

Social surveys, then, used locally, are a key mechanism for measuring the extent of criminal victimization, people's concerns about that criminal victimization, and how policy responses might be formulated in order to respond to those concerns. For left realism, using the social survey in a geographically focused and local way, provides a mechanism for contextualizing people's fears without either downplaying them through the production of aggregate statistical representations or by making any necessary prior presumption concerning the level of rationality to be attributed to those worries or concerns. Such surveys also provide a database from which to construct some notion of democratic output.

Social surveys offer the opportunity of gathering some measure of understanding of the public's priorities with respect to crimework. Of course, those priorities will not be expressed as universal concerns. However, without such an input, left realists would argue that policy makers have no clear sense of direction around those initiatives for which public support can be mobilized and those initiatives for which public support might need to be differently harnessed, and for which sections of the public. The principle of democratic output recognizes that not only does the public have a role to play in formulating and shaping crime policy but also it has a role to play in its effective implementation, alongside both the formal and the informal agencies in any particular community. In other words, the process of crime control policy and its implementation is complex, the success of which may be dependent upon the quality of the relationships formed between policy makers, members of the crime control industry, and the general public.

Consequently, looking for simple cause and effect solutions in relations to crime prevention may be misplaced; the best to be hoped for in the short term may be marginal gains rather than dramatic changes (a clear point of convergence between left realism and right realism). Taking the needs of local people seriously may produce unmeasurable but nevertheless qualitative improvements on the local quality of life none of which may be ultimately reflected in the crime statistics. This does not mean that a locally constructed and locally informed intervention has not worked. It does mean, however, that it may make little sense to use crime statistics as a measure of effectiveness. This view reflects a further left realist principle: the principle of democratic measurement.

For the left realist, as for many other strands of criminology, criminal statistics, as a source of information about the nature and extent of criminal behaviour are hugely problematic. Moreover, the data derived from criminal victimization surveys do little to overcome the underlying problems associated with criminal statistics. It is necessary to appreciate that

> If Quetelet pointed to the existence of a dark figure of crime, realist and feminist studies have pointed to how this dark figure is qualitatively structured. The dark figure varies with what type of crime committed by whom against which victim. Such an analysis takes us one step further. The dark figure expands and contracts with the values we bring to our study: recent studies of the extent of marital rape or changes in child abuse over time clearly indicate this.
>
> (J. Young, 1992: 58)

However, the fact that we cannot measure the nature and extent of crime precisely as an 'objective' problem out there does not mean that there are not some features of that problem around which people are, or can be, unified and/or mobilized. So as J. Young (1992: 58) goes on to state, realism sees crime as a unifier, as a social democratic issue, rather like health and education around which some democratic principles can be constructed, since, as with health and education, the poor suffer the most from the problems associated with criminal behaviour. Such a 'unity of interest allows us the possibility, both of a common measuring rod, and a political base which can argue for taking crime seriously' (J. Young, 1992: 59). This leads us to the final principle of left realism: the principle of theory and practice.

Left realism challenges the conventional social scientific presumption that what takes place in academia can be and should be separated and separable from what takes place in the political and policy domains. Left realism recognizes that the practice of doing research is imbued with the personal theoretical and political preferences of the researcher if not the funder of such research; this is as much the case, for qualitative as for quantitative research; this being the case, it should be recognized and built into the research process. Moreover he goes on to argue that the same issues of political and personal commitment inform the policy making process and that nowhere is this more the case than in the realm of crime prevention. At the same time very few crime prevention initiatives are monitored for their effectiveness.

Recognition of these features of the reality of the research and policy making processes foregrounds the political commitments which underpin those processes and opens them up for further evaluation and debate. This view of these processes constitutes a further expression of the political views which underpin left realism – that of social democracy. The commitment by left realists to the principles of the social democratic process arguably informs all the other 'points of realism' outlined here. It is also arguably this direct espousal of such a commitment which has served to provoke the debate which left realism has generated and which is discussed below.

Taking crime and people seriously, then, not only involves acceptance of the value of a particular explanatory framework at a theoretical level and the more specific propositions which might flow from this, but also involves the acceptance of a particular political view of social reality and how the crime problem might best be prioritized and managed in the light of that political commitment. The extent to which this theory, practice, and the linking methodological strategies proposed by left realism, knit together has been subjected to quite close critical scrutiny. It is to a consideration of that critical scrutiny that we shall now turn.

Left realism UK style: a critique

The overtly political stance adopted by those committed to the principles of left realism, evidenced by the clearly stated desire to reclaim the law and order debate in the 1980s for the Labour Party, constituted one of the more obvious critical starting points for some commentators on these theoretical developments. For example, in reviewing some of the empirical findings emanating from left realist work, Brogden *et al.* (1988: 181–90) point to the way in which the political commitment of early left realist work led to an overreading of their own survey findings and go on to state that:

> The truth is that whilst it would be nice (and convenient) to think that complex public policies could be based directly on people's experiences, perceptions and attitudes, it is anything but realistic. The reality is that people's limited experiences, unreconstructed perceptions and shifting attitudes do not translate immediately and unproblematically into socially just policies – even if a survey could get at them accurately.
>
> (Brogden *et al.*, 1988: 189)

A number of related issues underpin this observation, issues which will provide the framework for the critical evaluation to be developed here. First, it raises the question of the relationship between theory and method. In other words to what extent has the left realist project managed to knit together its conceptual framework with an appropriate exploratory empirical agenda. This question of methodology (as opposed to research method) will lead us to extract a further issue of a more philosophical nature: what is meant by realism in this context? Second, it raises the questions of how do you make sense of survey data, how in that sense making process might policies be formulated and what might those policies look like? Third, it raises the question of what it is that people know about their own experiences of criminal victimization, and how might those experiences be best explored and made sense of? Though not explicit in the quote referred to above, this question is particularly pertinent to exploring the left realist claim to have embraced feminism.

Taken together these issues, while not exhaustive of the full range of criticisms to be made of the left realist project, will nevertheless provide a useful vehicle through which to explore its main strengths and weaknesses. Each in a different way raise fundamental questions, not only about the political possibilities of the ideas under discussion here, but also what is presumed in those ideas about the nature of human beings, crime as a concept, the causation of crime, and the possibilities of the general criminological enterprise. Before unpacking those presumptions in a little more detail we shall examine each of the questions outlined above in turn.

The question of methodology

The way in which any researcher presumes to connect their theoretical perspective with a particular way of exploring that theoretical perspective empirically, either implicitly or explicitly adopts a way of thinking about how and what kind of knowledge can be gathered about social reality. These ways of thinking about the knowledge gathering process structure, in a fundamental way, what it is that we think can be known about the world and the possibilities of accessing that knowledge. The label positivism, much criticized within criminology (see, for example, Taylor *et al.*, 1973) articulates one set of presumptions about the knowledge gathering process. Realism articulates another.

What is meant by realism, like what is meant by positivism, is open to interpretation. It is possible, however, to construct an understanding of the central features of a realist project by drawing on the work of Bhaskar and Giddens. In a fairly clear and succinct definition of realism, Outhwaite offers this illustration from the work of Bhaskar:

> The conception I am proposing is that people, in their conscious activity, for the most part unconsciously reproduce (and occasionally transform) the structures governing their substantive activities of production. Thus people do not marry to reproduce the nuclear family or work to sustain the capitalist economy. Yet it is nevertheless the unintended consequence (and inexorable result) of, as it is also a necessary condition for, their activity.
>
> (Outhwaite, 1987: 51)

What is intended to be made explicit here is the way in which the routine activities of individuals, more or less consciously engaged in, are structured by and through underlying social processes. These processes can be both sustained and threatened in the way in which individuals, acting as individuals or in concert with others, engage in their routine daily lives, not always aware of the underlying structures which inform those routine activities themselves. These underlying structures are what Bhaskar (1978) refers to as generative mechanisms. Such mechanisms can be both unobserved and unobservable, yet are real in their consequences (like the notion of the nuclear family, or an economic system called capitalism). Positing the existence of generative mechanisms, implies that in order to engage in any empirical investigation of the social world, it is necessary to go beyond the 'mere appearance' of social reality. It is necessary also to make sense of the underlying structures which result in those appearances. If this constitutes a way of thinking about the knowledge production process which can reasonably be identified as realist, the question remains as to whether 'left realism' resonates with such a view.

As was stated above, left realism starts from the theoretical position that we should take seriously those issues which people define as being serious and develop an understanding of social problems as people experience them. This places the victim and/or the potential victim of crime at the centre of the criminological stage at least in relation to formulating an appreciation of the experience of crime. The way in which those experiences have, to date, been explored empirically has been through the use of the criminal victimization survey. As was indicated above, the use of this survey has been geographically focused. However, the question at issue here is not with the way in which this measurement tool has been deployed but with the question of its appropriateness. Put another way, if realism as a methodology, is concerned to locate people's experiences within a social reality in which they will be more or less aware of the processes contributing to those experiences (as discussed above) then can the criminal victimization survey tap such concerns?

Criminal victimization surveys, whether used nationally or locally, face a number of difficulties in the process of implementation which challenge their accuracy as measuring instruments. This much is well known. However, the general difficulties associated with the utilization of the survey technique in this way are compounded when, on the one hand, a claim is made to take people's grievances seriously as well as on the other hand to locate those grievances within their material context. The social survey as a research instrument cannot achieve this. It can only capture the responses made by individuals to the particular questions asked at a particular moment in time. To claim any more from the survey method reflects a tendency to 'reduce agents to the bearers of structures' (Outhwaite, 1987: 111). Yet this is precisely what left realism appears to do. Not only does this apparent conflation of the relationship between the individual expression of experiences and the underlying structural processes occur, but also it has on occasion been presented as if this were non-problematic.

For example, Crawford *et al*. (1990) state that

> The social survey is a democratic instrument; it provides an accurate appraisal of people's fear, of their experience of victimization; it enables the public to express their assessment of police and public authority effectiveness and their doubts about the extent to which the police stay within the boundaries of the rule of law. If we are to view the public as a consumer, as Sir Peter Imbert most usefully suggests, then the social survey provides a detailed picture of consumer demands and satisfaction.
>
> (Crawford *et al*., 1990: 153)

This commitment to the social survey as a democratic instrument, as evidenced in the quote above and in the earlier discussion of the principles underpinning left realism, clearly conveys the methodological tension under discussion here. To elucidate, Galtung (1967) regarded the social survey as possessing one key vice. They suffered from an individualistic and democratic bias. Galtung's point was that, while social surveys do give everyone who participates in them a voice (that is their individual responses are all given the same weight), social reality is not simply the sum of these voices. It will be useful, perhaps, to explore this a little more fully.

Surveys make several assumptions. If we use the language of Sir Peter

Imbert, the then Commissioner of the Metropolitan Police, surveys assume that consumers are in a position to know social reality, that they can perceive that social reality accurately, and that those perceptions can be accurately articulated through the questions asked by the survey. Moreover, it is further presumed that a policy agenda can be reasonably constructed from this process. All of these assumptions point to the problem of not only how and what weight can be given to individual responses to a range of standardized questions, but how is it possible to make sense of those responses when indeed the nature of the data hides the fundamentally unequal nature of the social world? In other words, the survey instrument cannot capture the generative mechanisms of which realism as a methodology speaks. This is not intended to imply that left realism has no commitment to understanding social reality and the way it is structured by age, class, gender and ethnicity. At a theoretical level this certainly is not the case. However, the question remains open as to how these variables are deemed to interact with each other.

The criminal victimization survey provides a range of empirical observations as to the effects of these variables; indeed, those surveys conducted under the umbrella of left realism have more than served the purpose of reminding policy makers that criminal victimization is not evenly distributed across the population or even within different parts of the population. They have also been successful at counting more incidents of the kinds of criminal victimization somewhat neglected by more conventional criminal victimization work (violence against women, and racial harassment, for example). But an understanding of how these empirical findings have been generated, arguably, has been politically asserted rather than empirically so.

The argument presented here is not intended to convey that 'left realists' are not themselves aware of the issues discussed above: Matthews and Young state

> Social positivism is imbued with a sense of the objective, the mechanical and the instantaneous. Realism, by stressing the role of human consciousness within determinant circumstances, as in the tradition of subcultural theory, denies all of this.
>
> (Matthews and Young, 1992: 7)

What is more to the point, however, is that acceptance of these inherent difficulties associated with social positivism is not merely overcome by stating an awareness of them. How such difficulties have been overcome needs also to be demonstrated; though as has been stated already (and as will be demonstrated further below), some of the work associated with left realism has clearly shown that the survey instrument can be sensitively and usefully deployed in the study of criminal victimization.

The question of policy

The methodological tensions outlined above raise general questions concerning what can be read legitimately from social survey data. Moreover, it is also clear that left realism has placed great emphasis on the use of social surveys as a major (though not exclusive) source of information from which (democratically) informed crime prevention policies might be formulated. Such a commitment to the policy making process constructed in this way raises both specific questions concerning how such a process might be implemented and more general questions concerning the kinds of policies which might be put in place. We shall address each of these questions in turn.

As Matthews and Young (1992: 15) freely admit, they have been accused of political populism, 'of merely moving from a public "commonsense" attitude to one of policy' (Mugford and O'Malley, 1990: 3). This view of their commitment to the use of the social survey to inform the policy making process is denied. It is argued that 'policy cannot be read off a computer print out of public opinion' (Mugford and O'Malley, 1990: 5). As was suggested above, individuals may be more or less aware of the social process and/or problems which routinely structure their lives. Given this limitation, how is such data to be read?

> The expert, the social analyst, therefore, has a vital role in contextualizing the problem of crime. First of all in mapping the problems and then putting the problems in context. In short, the analyst uncovers problems and then gives weight to their severity. This is a basis for a rational input into the system of crime control.
>
> (Crawford *et al.*, 1990: 161)

In order for priorities to be realistically assessed it is necessary to take account of three factors: public priorities, the prevalence of each kind of crime, and an assessment of each crime's impact (J. Young, 1992: 43). Matthews and Young (1992: 16) go on to assert, 'on a political level this [process] involves a debate between the criminological expert and the public'.

It would be difficult to deny the importance of the need for public debate concerning appropriate criminal justice policy. Such a debate, appropriately informed, may provide the basis from which it is possible to construct a vision of what makes 'good' sense from that which is rooted in 'common' sense. In other words, 'victims are not always the best judge of an appropriate and just crime control policy' (Brogden *et al.*, 1988: 189) and, moreover, are not the only consumers of the criminal justice system (Jefferson *et al.*, 1992). The impasse here lies not so much with the question of the need for debate, but how that debate is to be constituted, by whom, and under what circumstances might the analyst lend greater weight to whose views? There are more than a few hints here of the Comtian view of the role of the social analyst (or social physician as Comte might have said), which is perhaps not surprising given the methodological tensions outlined above.

So the commitment to the use of the social survey as a social democratic instrument for informing the policy making process raises further questions concerning how that policy making process might be managed. Of course, what underpins these questions in a much more fundamental way is the left realist commitment to the integration of theory and practice, that is, a clear statement which ties the criminological enterprise to the policy making process. As Young and Matthews (1992: 10) state, 'ideas do not arise out of thin air, and that practical engagement on whatever level, is a crucial component in forming, testing, and shaping ideas'. As a principle, this is not so problematic. As a practice, of course, it is not so straightforward. Indeed, in some respects it could be argued that the kinds of policy suggestions which have emanated from left realism – multi-agency cooperation, greater use of community alternatives for dealing with offenders, recognition of the need to re-form the relationship between social rights and social obligations – did not need empirical evidence from expensive social surveys for such proposals to make 'good' sense in particular circumstances. Moreover, as Stenson and Brearly (1989: 3) argue, the 'theoretical bias towards methodological individualism creates the risk that it will be increasingly drawn into the methodological individualistic, utilitarian discourses which have long dominated state sponsored criminology and crime control policy'.

As the policy proposals alluded to above illustrate and as Sim *et al.* (1987: 59) state, the policies which flow from the left realist position 'accept rather than challenge the terrain of the powerful' and remain 'politically conservative in its conclusions about what can be done about the state'. This leads Downes and Rock (1988: 309–10) to observe that many of the policy suggestions emanating from left realism are not that far removed from those emanating from the more liberal sections of the Home Office. It is at this level that the tensions between what is politically valued and whether or not that is supported empirically re-emerge. It is also at this level that the question of whether or not left realism has or can capture social reality also re-emerges. These questions leave untouched the thorny issue of social power and how social power is both mediated by and hidden from individuals.

The question of feminism

While the party political allegiances of left realism have constituted a contentious source of criticism for the realist project, it is arguably politics of another kind which raised much more fundamental questions about left realist concerns. There are (at least) two questions raised by feminist work for the left realist project – one conceptual, one methodological. Can the concepts employed by victim-oriented research adequately capture and convey women's experiences of criminal victimization, and can the techniques chosen to measure those experiences adequately do so? Young (1988) claims that the local crime survey approach adopted by left realism takes on board the questions raised by the feminist movement concerning the nature and extent of the criminal victimization of women. This, he argues, is achieved in the following way.

First, it must be recognized that much of the actual impact of crime on women is trivialized and hence concealed. This concealment is then compounded by the levels of sexual harassment which women experience on a day to day basis, which, given the relative powerlessness of women, makes them more unequal victims and therefore vulnerable. All of these processes are framed by the way in which crime is ultimately constructed within a particular set of social relationships: patriarchy. These are the mechanisms, then, which underpin women's victimization and which the local, theoretically informed, crime survey (it is argued) can uncover. The question remains as to whether or not the kind of conceptual outline and research strategy offered here can achieve these aims.

Of course, surveys can and do uncover more incidents of whatever is being measured dependent upon how the questions are asked and of whom they are asked. So as Stanley and Wise rightly suggest

> If we wanted to 'prove' how terribly violent women's lives were, we'd go to women who live in violent places – run-down inner-city areas of large conurbations – who have actually experienced male violence and ask them about it . . . However if we called this a 'survey', then, with exemplary motives and using 'scientific means', 'the problem for those women out there' could be generalized into 'the problem for all women everywhere'.
>
> (Stanley and Wise, 1987: 110–11)

As this quote implies, it is not the method employed which guarantees feminist insight, but the conceptual framework in which that method has been utilized. This does not mean that social surveys and feminism do not mix. The work conducted by Russell (1990), Painter (1991) and Mooney (1993) clearly indicates that they do. What makes the use of the survey by these researchers feminist is theory. Moreover, social surveys cannot capture social processes which arguably form the basis of understanding what it is that women (or any other powerless group) see and experience as criminal victimization and what they do not. The question of feminism draws together in a rather neat way the two other tensions of methodology and policy discussed here, and it will be of value to follow those tensions through with a particular example.

Kinsey *et al.* (1986) argue for a policy agenda of minimal policing based on what the public wants. In this argument an exception is made for domestic disputes. The case is made, quite rightly, that there is a material base to the victimization of women which the criminal justice system has a role to challenge. While such a material base for women's experiences might make sense for some women, if a policy strategy is to be formulated based on what the community wants, there is no guarantee that the community, made up of men and women, will necessarily recognize, define and agree with making an exception for domestic disputes and thereby argue for more police intervention in this particular area. (This argument is developed by Dekeseredy and Schwartz, 1991.) This, arguably, is the resultant effect of the problem of 'standpoint' (Cain, 1986: 259).

It was suggested earlier that left realism asserted the importance of the variables of class, race, age and gender, and yet has failed to explore how these variables might interconnect with one another. For some (see for example, Edwards, 1989), this has resulted in the implicit (if not explicit) privileging of social class as an explanatory variable at the potential expense of other structuring relationships. The failure of left realists to engage reflexively in this way with their own practices makes it difficult for left realism 'to see or know from two different sites at once' (Cain, 1986: 261), that is, also to see gender. This is not to deny that empirically individuals, and/or individuals acting in concert, may occupy more than one empirical site, as Matthews and Young (1992) quite rightly observe. Cain's point, however, is more than an empirical one. This is a question of how to theorize those interconnections through the strategies of reflexivity, deconstruction and reconstruction (Cain, 1990b).

These three sources of criticism reflect a major underlying tension deeply embedded in the left realist project. That tension has been articulated by a number of different writers in terms of the assumptions which underpin the left realist use of the concept of crime and the role of a discipline called criminology. It is a tension which is constituted primarily in the binary relationship which is presumed to exist between modernism and postmodernism, a relationship which it is argued fundamentally challenges the possibility of there being something called criminology at all. However, before considering the questions posed by this debate for left realism it will be of some value to examine the form and content of other strands of criminology which might claim the label 'left realist'.

Left realism US style

The ideas associated with left realism have generated considerable debate and criminological attention in other countries outside of the UK. Proponents of versions of left realist ideas can be found in Australia, Canada and the United States. These versions of left realism have been careful to maintain the need for a context specific application of left realist ideas in different national and cultural settings. Brown and Hogg (1992) offer qualified support for the left realist project in Australia and MacLean (1992) provides a detailed empirical agenda and argument for the use of local crime surveys in Canada. While these developments carry with them explicit criticisms of the left realist project, they nevertheless adhere to the general political persuasion contained therein. In a similar way there was some early qualified support in the United States for taking crime seriously resonant with the concerns of Young and others in the UK. However, perhaps the most clearly articulated of all these international versions of left realism is that found in the work of Elliott Currie (1985).

During the 1980s the parallels between the UK and the USA in social and political terms were in some respects remarkable. The emulation and influence of American politics and policies was, of course, grounded in earlier decades, but that emulation arguably reached a new peak in the form of the political relationship which developed between Ronald Reagan and Margaret Thatcher during the 1980s. The similarity between these two leaders in the kinds of economic and political strategies adopted to respond to the world's changing economic climate contributed to, what appeared to be, an increasing desire to look for solutions to UK social problems in the United States. That same shared social and political climate also, arguably, contributed to the emergence of a similar debate to that found in the UK, both within academic criminology and within the sphere of criminal justice policy, as to how best to tackle the increasing crime problem. In the USA a major exponent of a left realist response to the crime problem was to be found in the work of Currie (1985). It will be valuable to consider Currie's arguments in order to develop our understanding of both the similarities and differences in what might be called a left realist criminology.

Currie's work, rather like that of Young's, emerged not only from the social and economic changes taking place in the USA (alluded to above), but also from a deep dissatisfaction with the (then) current mainstream criminological thought. He considered that the conservative explanation of crime was unhelpful for two reasons. First theoretically, to say that the propensity to commit crime is part of human nature, meaning that some people are just more evil than others, ignores the huge differences in crime rates in different areas. Second in policy terms, to say that if you increase the costs of crime (that is if you lock more people up for longer) ignores the question of whether or not locking people up actually makes a difference. Currie also argues that liberal criminology had offered no effective alternative to such conservative thinking, again for two reasons stemming from the failure of that criminological viewpoint to appreciate the depth of the social and personal impact that crime has. First, liberal criminology failed to appreciate the complexity of political economy and has thus avoided the difficult issue of just how do you create jobs. Second, liberal criminology failed to appreciate the complexity of communities in which crime prevention strategies had been more often than not couched in individualistic terms.

From a thoroughgoing analysis and critique of the political and policy possibilities of both conservative and liberal criminology, Currie constructs his own analysis and policy agenda towards a better management of the crime problem. For Currie (1985) work is the central bond which links people to society. In a later piece he argues that it is the economic problem of producing too much (overcapacity) sustained in the 1990s by what he calls the 'jobless recovery' (that is an economy recovery which did not involve creating more jobs) alongside the political expectation that there are private solutions to the consequences of these processes which expresses the central importance of this bond.

> In the long run there can be no private sector solution to the crisis of over-capacity. Nor therefore a private sector solution to the inevitable social crises which that trend is already bringing and which will worsen in the future. Namely mass exclusion from meaningful work; the resulting declining income and social well being; rising poverty among increasing numbers denied access to livelihood, and a widening gulf between them and those who are able to cling to the remaining stable and well rewarded jobs; social pathology and social conflict on an unprecedented scale.
>
> (Currie, 1995: 72)

Centring the need for work in this way, and identifying the underlying mechanisms which have changed, fundamentally and on a world wide basis, the nature of work, constitutes the key theoretical focus from which Currie's more specific policy agenda emanates. That agenda is worth focusing on in some detail.

Currie (1985) recommends:

- a stronger response to domestic violence by the police and the courts
- greater attention to be paid to innovative policing practices
- greater use of more middle range sanctions by the courts
- the development of intensive rehabilitation programmes for young offenders, preferably in the community or a supportive institutional setting
- community based, comprehensive family support programmes
- improved family planning and support for teenage parents
- paid leave and more accessible childcare to ease the conflicts between work and home
- high quality, early education for the disadvantaged
- an expansion of the community dispute resolution programme
- local services for victims of domestic violence
- intensive job training for the young
- upgrading low paid jobs
- a permanent job creation programme
- universal and generous income support for families headed by individuals outside the labour force.

(Currie, 1985: 275–6)

The criminological thinking underpinning a policy agenda such as this involves taking seriously the impact of crime, especially the impact of violent crime on women. In addition it also involves taking seriously the fundamental features of a society which bind that society together, namely the world of work and the diversity of family structures which support and sustain individuals as they participate in the wider social order. Currie's agenda does not pathologize those who are not members of the labour force or those for whom the notion of the nuclear family has little resonance. But his agenda does involve taking seriously that evidence which connects family life and joblessness with the likelihood of engaging in criminal behaviour and constructing policy response which might (realistically?) tackle such issues.

In some respects Currie's realism, as wide ranging as it is, might in a UK political context look more like idealism. Nevertheless, there are specific points of overlap between this agenda and that proposed by left realism in the UK. In particular the emphasis on the role of the police, community alternatives to punishment and a concern with violence against women are the obvious points of comparison. So too are the dissatisfactions expressed with the way in which the criminological enterprise has respectively understood and offered proposals on the crime problem, as is their respective concern to take the impact of crime seriously, especially the way that impact takes its toll on the socially disadvantaged. Currie's focus on understanding the changing nature of work and the differing ways in which individuals connect with that world, however, stands somewhat in marked contrast with the emphasis on relative deprivation found in the work of Young. These are not, of course, mutually exclusive concerns, but arguably, Currie's deeper concern with the role of political economy equips us with a clearer conceptualization of his vision of the underlying generative mechanisms producing a range of social problems, without the necessity for local crime surveys to support his analysis!

In this particular contextual evaluation of left realism Currie's work also exposes the criminological left wing continuities with the earlier radical tradition of Marxism. This commitment is not so easily identifiable in the writings of realists in the UK, though some have observed that the policy proposals emanating from the work of Young are discernible in the last chapter of *The New Criminology* (Taylor *et al.*, 1973). It is a commitment, however, which returns us to some of the more fundamental and uneasy tensions embedded in the left realist commitment to a fairly traditional interpretation of the nature of criminology and its subject matter: the modernist dilemma.

The problem of modernism

Matthews and Young (1992) commit themselves unashamedly to the modernist project. This much is clear. Yet such a commitment does not offer a complete answer to those critics who draw attention to the problems of treating crime as a unified and unifying concept, treating the notion of the victim in the same way, and the underlying essentialist and totalizing presumptions that these practices lead to. We shall address each of these questions in turn.

These problems raise, in a different way, the explicit commitment to the interconnection between theory and politics found within the left realist project. In that commitment common sense, everyday understandings of crime are treated as if such understandings were by definition non-problematic. In other words, taking seriously how people define and understand their experiences as the starting point of criminological investigation treats those definitions and experiences as though 'there is an easily recognisable reality "out there", known as crime, that can be understood through empirical investigation and in its own terms' (Carlen, 1992: 59).

Not only is the presumption made that crime can be identified in this way but also it is presumed that through understanding crime in this way consensual support can be galvanized for policy change.

> The uncritical use of the concept 'crime' suggests that other purposes may underlie the realist project, or at least that it does not escape the effects of a certain essentialism − an essentialism that utilises crime as an ideological unifier: a mode for expressing the 'real' and common interests of working-class people.
>
> (Brown and Hogg, 1992: 145)

This uncritical use of the concept of crime therefore has two problematic elements associated with it: one empirical (the presumption that there is some steadfast and easily identifiable empirical referent out there called 'crime'), and one political, that such an empirical referent resonates with the 'natural' supporters of the Labour Party whose attitudes towards criminal justice policy are also, coincidentally, progressive.

Invoking the concept of crime in this way not only overlooks the problems inherent in assuming that common sense articulated a social reality 'out there' rather than one which is socially constructed, and commonly understood. It also overlooks the problem of how that common sense is to be transformed into something identifiably progressive; it takes little imagination to identify some aspects of common sense which could hardly be identified as progressive at all. So while 'left realism' on the one hand within its basic principles reflects a concern with specificity − a desire to be locally sensitive to locally informed policy solutions − its underlying commitment to modernism, demonstrated by its unproblematic use of the terms crime, victim, and so on clearly militate against its ability to achieve this goal. Locally informed policy agendas might not be progressive at all.

The question of the relationship between the left realist commitment to the modernist project, so deeply embedded in the criminological enterprise, raises questions about the nature of criminology as a whole. It is a question raised for all the social sciences by postmodernism. Put simply, postmodernism asks: is it at all possible to talk in universal terms, to make claims concerning truth? Can there be anything deemed as 'knowledge' above and beyond experience? Expressed in this way treating the notion of 'crime' as though it represented some unifying and essential concept, is problematic indeed.

Conclusion

This chapter has offered a relatively detailed overview of both the form and the content of that version of criminological theorizing known as 'left realism'. In offering this overview particular attention has been paid not only to its strengths and limitations in constituting a theoretical and empirical agenda for criminology, but also to its variant forms. Indeed, it is within those variant forms and some of the more fundamental criticisms of the 'left realist' project that it is possible to catch sight of other ways of thinking about the criminological enterprise. For this author there are two problematic issues endemic to the 'left realist' project which demand reconciliation in one form or another if a genuine alternative (left wing?) criminological agenda is to be constructed. The first issue relates to the question of what constitutes the real. The second issue is concerned with the relevance of postmodernism. We shall deal with each of these issues in turn.

Arguably, it is the question of what constitutes the real which, at a fundamental level, most clearly delineates the left realism of Currie from the left realism of Young. In this chapter that has been most definitively articulated in Currie's concern with the relationship between the changing nature of the political economy and the impact that has on people's lives (including crime) and Young's focus on the concept of 'relative deprivation'. Here we are presented with two analyses, both claiming a left wing position, with each arguably presenting the cause of crime as being constituted at different levels. These are, of course, not mutually exclusive positions. But in comparing the two, Currie's analysis comes closer to identifying a way of understanding how the real is constituted which resonates more readily with a Bhaskarian definition of realism. If Bhaskarian realism does offer a way of thinking about how the real is constituted, then such a framework provides a much more effective mechanism of exploring the ways in which the various points on the 'square of crime' not only relate to each other but are also fundamentally constituted in and by processes outside the question of crime and the workings of the criminal justice system. There are different ways in which developing an understanding of those interconnections might be constructed. One way is offered in Chapters 5 and 6.

The second fundamental issue raised in this chapter is that concerning criminology's relationship with and intimate connection to the modernist project and the questions that postmodernism raise for this relationship. As was stated earlier, postmodernism poses a fundamental challenge to the domain assumptions of all the social sciences, not just criminology. Some of that challenge for criminology has been at its most pertinent in the work emanating from feminism, some of which is discussed in Chapter 5. Others, however, have endeavoured to take the postmodernist challenge on board and to construct a 'criminology' informed by these ideas. The likely success of such an enterprise is open to dispute. A consideration of the relevance of some of these ideas is, however, offered in Chapter 8.

To summarize: Young (1994) is correct to point out the clear points of convergence between right realism and left realism especially in their respective starting points – the desire to take crime and the crime problem seriously. It is also useful to observe that, in the context of the UK at least, there is a much more clearly identifiable body of knowledge and work labelled left realism. That body of knowledge and work has certainly shifted the academic agenda and contributed to the policy one both locally and nationally. In this respect, it may be that left realism has met some of its goals. It remains to be seen how effective those shifts may or may not have been in adding to a better understanding of crime and the crime problem.

Further reading

The best source for understanding left realism and the criticism it has generated are the two collections of papers edited by Matthews and Young. These are *Issues in Realist Criminology* (Matthews and Young, 1992) and *Rethinking Criminology: The Realist Debate* (Young and Matthews, 1992).

chapter five

Gendering the criminal

In Chapter 1 an attempt was made to explore some of the tensions between criminological talk about crime and common-sense talk about crime. In so doing it was suggested that there was some tension between that which criminologists took to be the 'truth', that which common sense took to be the 'truth', and what is made both visible and invisible in both of these 'truths'. One issue around which both criminology and common sense have been relatively blind is the question of gender. In this chapter we shall explore the way in which gender issues have been hidden by criminology, the different ways in which feminists have attempted to make those issues visible, and the more recent interest in the maleness of crime. This interest has emerged largely independently of the concerns outlined in Chapters 3 and 4. But first, how has the question of *gender* as opposed to sex been hidden within criminology?

The gender blindness of criminology

Braithwaite (1989: 44) suggests that the first 'fact' that any theory of crime should fit is that crime is disproportionately committed by males. In 1992, for example, of all those found guilty of or cautioned for, indictable offences, 81 per cent were males and 19 per cent were females (Criminal Statistics for England and Wales, 1993). Moreover, it is possible to argue that if account is taken of the findings of feminist-inspired work on rape and domestic violence (crimes which are still frequently hidden and also disproportionately committed by men), then the maleness of crime is heightened. Yet the early incursions into criminology made by feminists were not so concerned to take account of or explain this maleness of crime as to talk about 'women and crime'.

This concern with 'women and crime' began with the seminal work of Smart (1977) and was continued by Leonard (1982), Heidensohn (1985), Morris (1987) and Naffine (1987). These texts shared a number of common concerns: to raise the visibility of women within criminological knowledge, to address women's relationship with crime not only as offenders but also as victims, to understand crime as a male dominated activity produced not as a result of sex differences but as a product of gender differences. However, many of these early texts tended to treat the 'woman and crime problem' as if it were a separate and separable issue within criminology. As Brown (1986) cogently argued, the more the woman question was treated in this way the more that mainstream (read *malestream*) criminology was left alone and presumed to have got its story straight on men. This stance carries with it a number of dangers, not least of which is the presumption that when we speak of gender this refers only to women and not to men. Moreover, as Smart's (1977) treatise suggests, a niche called 'women and crime' might also further perpetuate the marginalization of gender-related questions and at the same time draw policy makers' attention to issues not necessarily in women's interests.

There is, however, a more fundamental question posed by a concern with just women and crime, and that question raises the issue of the whole relationship between feminism and criminology. Gelsthorpe and Morris (1990), for example, choose to talk of feminist *perspectives* and criminology arguing that:

> Criminology has for many feminist writers and researchers been a constraining rather than a constructive and creative influence. Indeed, in a sense our task in this book is to fracture its boundaries.
>
> (Gelsthorpe and Morris, 1990: 2)

So what are these feminist perspectives of which Gelsthorpe and Morris speak and how have they influenced criminology, if at all, and how might they differently gender criminology?

Feminism and criminology

There are four identifiable strands to feminist thought, all of which have had a different impact on criminology: liberal feminism, radical feminism, socialist feminism and postmodern feminism. We shall discuss the differential influence of each of these in turn.

Liberal feminism

Liberal feminism, stemming from the work of Wollstonecraft, Taylor and Mill, presumes that it is 'bad' or 'poor' scientific practice which produces the sexist bias in empirical research. In other words, it is a view of the scientific process which presumes that the rules of science and scientific inquiry are in themselves sound; what is at fault is how they are applied. To alleviate this problem liberal feminists align themselves with the view that more women researchers are needed, and that any empirical investigation should include women in the sample.

In some respects it is possible to argue that liberal feminism has had the longest historical impact on the study of criminology. This statement can be defended in a number of ways. First, there have always been women researchers looking at the problems associated with crime. There may not have been very many of them, and the work that they produced may not have been particularly radical, but they were nevertheless present and they were examining the sex differentials associated with crime, especially delinquency (see, for example, Glueck and Glueck, 1950; Wootton, 1959; Cowie *et al.*, 1968). In other words, there is both a history of women researching within criminology and a history of work addressing female offending behaviour.

It is possible to align much of that work with the liberal imperative of ensuring that females feature as a part of any empirical data set – a question of good 'scientific' practice. There is a second theme, however, to that work which we might locate as being influenced by liberal feminism – a focus on the discriminatory practices of the criminal justice system. This strand reveals itself in different ways.

Arguably the work of Pollak (1950), concerned as it was with understanding the influence that chivalry might play in the under-documenting of women's criminality, is at the same time a study of discriminatory practice. The presumption that women are discriminated against, either favourably or unfavourably, within the criminal justice system has informed a wealth of criminological research. Research has shown that factors such as type of offence (Hindelang, 1979; Farrington and Morris, 1983), home circumstances (Datesmann and Scarpitti, 1980) and personal demeanour (DeFleur, 1975) are contributory factors to the way in which women are processed by the criminal justice system.

This theme has been explored in ever more detailed and specific circumstances; in magistrate's courts (Eaton, 1986), in prison (Carlen, 1983; Dobash *et al.*, 1986) and in women's experiences as victims of crime (Chambers and Millar, 1983; Edwards, 1989). That these factors simply represent sexist practices, however, is not easy to assert. Some studies suggest that women are treated more leniently by the courts, others suggest a harsher outcome. Such contradictory conclusions point to the complex way in which factors such as age, class, race, marital status and previous criminal record interact with each other. Moreover, Gelsthorpe (1989) found that there were organizational influences which affected the way in which females were dealt with by practitioners which were difficult to attribute to sexist or discriminatory practices alone.

Gelsthorpe (1989) goes on to discuss the key drawbacks to this anti-discriminatory theme within criminological work. First, it assumes that women have been neglected systematically by criminology whereas it might be more accurate to assert that criminological concerns have developed rather more erratically than this. Women were the focus of some early criminological work (as suggested above). Moreover, women are not the only blind spot within criminology. There are others, such as, for example, race. Second, the focus on sexism presumes that if criminological theory and/or practices were emptied of sexism, then the theories and the practices would in themselves prove to be sound. This presumption, of course, returns us to one of the key problematics of liberal feminism; the fact that it leaves unchallenged what the yardsticks against which our understandings are measured. Third, much of this work assumes that sexism applies only to women. Gelsthorpe argues that this is an 'untenable' assumption; what about men? Finally, the complexity of the findings in this area do make it difficult to assert which outcomes are a result of direct discrimination.

Some writers have argued that the pursuit of this discriminatory theme, with its underpinning assumption of equality before the law is no longer a fruitful enterprise for feminists interested in the crime problem (Smart, 1990). What is clear, however, is that the work informed by these themes has yielded a wealth of information concerning the complex way in which factors interact to produce different outcomes for different female offenders and victims of crime. Indeed, it is the sheer weight of that evidence which renders a simplistic assertion of chivalry highly problematic and points to understanding women's experiences of the criminal justice system by reference to factors outside the operation of the criminal justice system.

Radical feminism

Understanding the ways in which such processes result in differential outcomes for victims of crime leads to a consideration of the value and impact of radical feminism on criminological concerns. In contrast to liberal feminism, radical feminism focuses more clearly on *men's* oppression of women rather than on other social conditions which might result in women's subordination. Crucial to the radical feminist analysis is the question of sexuality. The emphasis within radical feminism on women's oppression and control through their sexuality has had its greatest impact on criminology through the avenue of 'victim studies'. It must be said, however, that radical feminists display a far greater preference for the term 'survivor' rather than 'victim', since that term implies a more positive and active role for women in their routine daily lives. These contentions over terminology, notwithstanding the work of radical feminists on rape (including marital rape and date rape), domestic violence, child abuse and sexual murder, have certainly constituted a challenge to criminology in what is defined as criminal, the extent of that criminality and its location. (See, for example, Stanko, 1985; Cameron and Fraser, 1987; Russell, 1990.)

Understanding and embracing the 'safe haven' of the home as a place in which much criminal behaviour occurs, and is perpetrated by men towards women, is still a difficulty for some mainstream (malestream) criminological work, since taking this seriously means taking gender seriously. The campaigning voice of radical feminism which shouts 'all men are potential rapists' reflects both the power and the threat of feminist studies to a criminology informed in this way. There are difficulties, however, with accepting this stance uncritically.

Radical feminism presumes that all men have the same power and control over their own lives as they have over women. Moreover, the view that 'All men are potential rapists' presumes that all men have the same relationship with violence and to the expression of their masculinity in violence towards women. This presumption is derived from the problem of essentialism of which radical feminism is frequently accused. Essentialism asserts the view that there are immutable differences between men and women shared by all men and all women. Moreover, while radical feminism, despite this problem, has centred on men's sexual oppression of women as a key criminological concern, sex is not the only variable about which criminology had had a blind spot. The complex ways in which variables such as sex, race or class might interact with one another has been the central concern of socialist feminism. Here some attention will be paid to the work of Messerschmidt (1986) as articulating one expression of this position.

Socialist feminism

Messerschmidt has this to say about his theoretical framework for understanding crime:

> My socialist feminist understanding of crime had two premises. First, to comprehend criminality (of both the powerless and the powerful) we

must consider simultaneously patriarchy and capitalism and their effects on human behaviour. Second from a social feminist perspective, power (in terms of gender and class) is central for understanding serious forms of criminality. It was theorised that the powerful (in both the gender and class spheres) do the most criminal damage to society. Further, the interaction of gender and class creates positions of power and powerlessness in the gender/class hierarchy, resulting in different types and degrees of criminality and varying opportunities for engaging in them. Just as the powerful have more legitimate opportunities, they also have more illegitimate opportunities.

(Messerschmidt, 1993: 56)

As Messerschmidt himself admits, as with all theoretical constructions, this framework has its limitations. For example, it denudes the criminal actor of a sense of agency, locating the motivation for crime within the social system. It also asserts patriarchy as being unitary and uniform in its impact on both men and women. Yet despite these problems this framework does offer a starting point which posits an understanding of criminality located within socio-structural conditions – a way of thinking about the criminal behaviour of both men and women and the way in which those socio-structural conditions impact upon men and women. Elements of these concerns are also found in the work of Carlen.

It is important to note that Carlen recognizes the importance of feminism as a politics rather than as a guarantor of theoretical or empirical truth (Carlen, 1990). Moreover, Carlen is very critical of feminist efforts at explaining criminal behaviour and points to two major limitations in such efforts with respect to female lawbreaking behaviour in particular. First, she argues that an exclusive focus on women's lawbreaking behaviour presumes that women break the law for essentially different reasons than men do. This, for Carlen, reflects a reductionist and essentializing position similar to that adopted by the biological positivists. Second, when the historically and socially specific contexts of male and female offending behaviours are examined, the explanatory concepts which emerge rapidly merge with issues of racism, classism and imperialism rather than gender *per se*.

She goes on to comment that women in prison represent those whose criminalization has been overdetermined by the threefold effects of racism, sexism and classism, none of which is reducible to the other and all of which, for Carlen, point to connecting the debate around women and crime to the broader issue of social justice.

What is particularly striking about both the theoretical work of Messerschmidt (1986) and the range of work conducted by Carlen, on female offenders and women in prison, is the way in which both these writers have drawn on conceptual formulations which take us outside of mainstream criminological debates in order to understand the nature of criminality. This process of moving to debates outside of criminology in order to understand women's and men's experiences of the criminal justice system is one of the features of what Cain (1990b: 2) has called 'transgressive criminology'.

Cain's 'transgressive criminology' constitutes a call to move beyond what she defines as the 'binding web of co-man sense' (Cain, 1990b: 8). In order to do this criminology must take seriously that which actors themselves take seriously yet simultaneously make visible that which is taken for granted. This concern generates a criminological shopping list of women only studies, that is studies exploring the totality of women's lives, as well as studies of men. As Cain (1990b: 12) states, criminology must take on board the question of 'what in the social construction of maleness is so profoundly criminogenic: why do males so disproportionately turn out to be criminals?'

There are clearly some parallels between the work of Carlen and Cain and the respective questions they raise for criminology. While Carlen would not concur with any particular claims to a *feminist* methodology and would eschew the term 'feminist' for all but campaigning purposes (in contrast to elements of Cain's work), their joint focus on locating gender issues as being just one dynamic of both women's and men's experiences of the criminal justice system and their concern to place those experiences within a broader social context outside of criminology, gives some flavour as to why each of them in different ways find the label 'feminist criminology' disturbing. Moreover, each in their different ways have also found it important to challenge any approach which endeavours to essentialize the differences between males and females, as found in radical feminism.

Postmodern feminism

Of all of the feminisms under discussion here it is perhaps fair to say that as yet postmodern feminism has had relatively little impact upon criminology. Put rather simply, postmodern feminism celebrates difference. It is a position which is concerned to address the positive side of being the 'other', that is, outside mainstream thinking and concerns. This 'otherness' for postmodern feminism represents openness, plurality, diversity and difference, and it is an emphasis which renders problematic any uncritical or universalizing use of the category 'women' or 'men' to denote all women or all men. In criminological terms, postmodernism attempts to give voice to those silenced by the discourses of modernism.

In order to do this within criminology, Alison Young (1992) argues that it is necessary to appreciate the power of criminology's 'semantic rectangle'. This reveals that the structure of the discipline of criminology is imbued with assumptions around two oppositional pairs: Normal/Criminal, Male/Female. These pairs subjugate the normal to the criminal, the male criminal to the female criminal, the female criminal to the criminal, the normal to the male criminal, etc. Thus, when the category 'criminal' is paired with the category 'male criminal' they are almost indistinguishable within criminology; when the category 'female criminal' is paired with the category 'normal', normality is subjugated. As Alison Young (1992: 76) states, 'Woman is always criminal, always deviant, always censured. This condition is utterly normal.'

So postmodern feminism demands that we go beyond the transgressive requirements of Cain. It demands not that we deny racism or sexual violence, but that we deny the view that the intellectual *per se* can devise any answers to these problems. This not only shakes the conceptual foundations on which criminology is based, but also shakes its assumed relevance and ability to produce Knowledge or Truth on which to make policy claims. This renders the notion of traditional empirical work and any associated policy agenda very problematic for postmodernism. As a consequence while this work has generated a highly provocative critique of criminology (see, for example, A. Young, 1992) it has generated little generalizable empirical knowledge. Indeed, such a product stands in contradiction to the postmodernist project.

The resistance found to postmodernist ideas within criminology does not mean that such ideas in general have not been influential in encouraging a reconsideration of the relationship between the social scientific search for knowledge and the claims that can be attached to such knowledge. It is clear that giving voice to diversity is an explicit concern of both of the agendas of Carlen and Cain, for example. Giving voice to that diversity has not only led to a reconsideration of the way in which feminism in general has presumed that the category 'woman' represents Women but also led to a re-examination of what is implied by the category 'man' and the way in which this has been used to delineate all Men. The blossoming literature on masculinity/masculinities stands testimony to this. However, before considering the value of that literature to criminology it will be useful to offer some assessment on the state of the relationship between the feminism outlined here and criminological knowledge.

Feminism and criminology: contradictions in terms?

The extent to which it might be possible to argue that feminism(s) and criminology constitute contradictions in terms depends to a certain extent on which of the feminisms is being discussed. Certainly liberal feminism with its concern to practise good science and to address discriminatory practices sits most comfortably with mainstream criminological concerns. In this brand of feminism the commitment to the central problems of criminology remain unchallenged; what criminology needs is more accurate knowledge about who commits crime and why. Radical feminism, on the other hand, sits much less comfortably with mainstream criminological concerns; indeed radical feminist work which has relevance for criminology has largely emerged outside of the criminological domain, though its importance for criminology lies in its concern to address men and their behaviour towards women. So the tensions which exist between this brand of feminism and criminology are largely dependent upon whether or not 'men' as men are considered the central concern of the criminological agenda.

Socialist feminism, however, takes us beyond a concern with just men and women towards addressing the ways in which a range of structural variables interact with one another to both enable and constrain the behaviours of men and women. Here again the tension with criminology lies not so much with the subject matter of crime itself but how the exploration of that subject matter might be best conceived.

Postmodern feminism poses the most fundamental challenge for criminology. The strains within postmodernism against any universal explanations towards contextualizing and specifying the differences between people renders the criminological implication in the policy making process highly problematic indeed.

So each of these feminisms poses different questions for criminology and genders criminology in quite different ways. More recently criminology has, arguably as a result of the work of both radical and socialist feminism, attempted to place men and masculinity more squarely on the criminological agenda. Before considering the extent to which the developments in criminological theory have or have not been influenced by the question of gender, we shall offer a brief overview of the differing ways in which the question of masculinity has been addressed and how that has been manifested within criminology.

Ways of thinking about men within criminology

Men certainly have not been absent from criminological thinking. Indeed the activities of young, urban males have preoccupied criminologists since the delinquency studies of the 1940s and 1950s. What criminologists have paid little attention to, however, are the potentially different ways in which the behaviour of young, urban males might be informed by their understanding of themselves as men: or indeed how criminological analyses might be better understood as a reflection of male understandings about crime! Here we shall offer a brief overview of how those understandings have become deeply embedded in the criminological literature.

In 1977 Tolson wrote a book entitled *The Limits of Masculinity*. In this book he explored the different ways in which dominant forms of thinking about masculinity constrained different men in different ways. In some ways Tolson's work constituted a central moment in setting the further development of the exploration of masculinity. His work posed two key questions for that debate. Is there one overarching form of masculinity or many, diverse masculinities? Is masculinity best understood as a product of sex role development or gender relations? These two questions have clearly underpinned the debate on masculinity which ensued during the 1990s. Each of them informs the summary which follows.

Sex role theory and criminology

The concept of role is central to social psychology and some versions of sociology. As a concept it is used as a way of organizing people's behaviour into a meaningful whole. It acts as a mechanism for understanding the ways in which social expectations, actions and behaviour reflect stereotypical assumptions about behavioural expectations; that is, what it is that should be done, by whom, and under what circumstances. In the context of understanding gender relations this leads to the identification of male roles and female roles. These roles are presumed to outline the appropriate behavioural sets and associated expectations for men and women (male(s) and female(s)). Sex role theory takes as given the biological origins which define the differences between males and females. These biological origins constitute the raw material onto which specific behavioural sets, called sex roles, are painted through the process of socialization. As a theory then it is rooted in essentially *biological* assumptions concerning what counts as the *defining* characteristics of being male and female.

In the criminological context the work of both Sutherland (1947) and Parsons (1937) embraced sex role theory. Indeed, these two writers have wielded a particular influence on criminology's grasp of the maleness of the crime problem so we shall examine briefly the work of each of them in turn.

Sutherland's key premise was that criminal behaviour was learned behaviour like any other. Moreover, he argued that people learned criminal behaviour when exposed to an 'excess of definitions' favouring deviant as opposed to conventional (or rule abiding) behaviour. This view of criminal behaviour focused on not only the importance of the socialization process in learning crime but also on understanding the importance of the values attached to the behaviour learned, meaning that it is not only a matter of who you associate with but also the kinds of meanings those associations provide for an individual with respect to engaging in criminal behaviour. So an individual may know how to act criminally, but may not do so in the absence of the values, motives, attitudes, etc., which support such behaviour. The more an individual is exposed to such support the more likely it is that an individual will share in that behaviour. For Sutherland, then, criminal behaviour was learned behaviour like any other behavioural response rather than being the product of some innate atavistic or degenerative drive.

Within this general framework Sutherland commented that boys were more likely to become delinquent than girls. This, he suggested, happened for two reasons. First, because boys are less strictly controlled by the socialization process in general than girls are. Second, because in that process they are taught to be tough, aggressive, active, risk seekers, all characteristics which Sutherland considered to be prerequisites for involvement in the criminal world. These two factors taken together mean that boys are more frequently exposed to the kinds of learning situations in which criminality becomes a possibility. This happens despite the fact that in other respects both boys and girls may be growing up together in the same economically deprived neighbourhoods, clearly indicative of a view that there is something more to be understood about boys' involvement in the criminal world than can be explained by reference to socio-economic factors alone.

This general theory of criminal behaviour was labelled by Sutherland (1947) as the theory of 'differential association'. When it is applied generally to an understanding of criminal behaviour it can be seen to offer a framework substantially different in some respects from that proposed by the biological positivists. However, when applied specifically to understanding the differences between male and female involvement in delinquent behaviour there are a number of issues which this theory treats as being unproblematic.

As a theory it is rooted in the presumption of sex role theory and thereby a notion of biological difference. Being rooted in this way it consequently accepts implicitly a view that biological difference constitutes part of the explanation for any observed behavioural differences, despite the foregrounding of the importance of the socialization process. It must be remembered that in sex role theory the socialization process only provides the mechanism through which specific learning takes place. In other words, the fact that girls, not boys, become pregnant constitutes the basis for explaining both their different experience of the socialization process and their subsequent different rate of criminality. This is particularly evident in that work influenced by functionalism. Indeed, the work of Parsons (1937) added a further dimension to this way of thinking about the relationship between sex differences, the socialization process and the maleness of criminal behaviour.

The functionalist sociology of Talcott Parsons placed the family at the centre of the social learning associated with sex roles. In the family, children learn that the expressive role, the role associated with nurturing, caring and keeping the family together, is what women do; the instrumental role, that concerned with achievement, goal attainment and breadwinning, is what men do. In the work of Parsons, these roles provide for the stability of society from one generation to the next. Moreover, society in general and the family in particular is presumed to operate most effectively in this form. This presumption is made on the basis of the fact that because women have the reproductive capacity to bear children they are thus deemed to be best suited for the expressive role, a role that is denied to men and which young men experience as being denied to them.

The process of learning these sex roles poses different problems for boys than for girls. Exposed to feminine care, girls have little difficulty in finding appropriate role models for themselves. Boys, on the other hand, do not have a readily and routinely available male model to follow. Exposed to the female model as young children, they quickly learn that the feminine role model is not one for which they will be accepted as men. Parsons (1937) argues, therefore, that boys engage in what he calls 'compensatory compulsory masculinity'. In other words, boys reject any behaviour seen to be feminine. So tenderness, gentleness and the expression of emotion are rejected because they are not seen to be masculine. In their place boys pursue that which they observe to be masculine – being powerful, tough, and rough. The pursuit of these masculine characteristics is engaged in vigorously, in order to avoid any doubt being cast on the boys' sense of themselves as men or of their being recognized by others as men. This pursuit of masculinity, and its approved forms of expression, results in boys engaging in anti-social behaviour much more often than girls. It is this greater likelihood to engage in anti-social behaviour which is subsequently related to their greater delinquency.

The work of Cohen (1955) draws together both the work of Sutherland and Parsons and was very influential in the development of delinquency studies during the 1950s and 1960s. Following Parsons, Cohen viewed the process of socialization in the home as neither a smooth nor an easy process for boys. He accepted the view that the lack of a readily available masculine role in the home, alongside the availability of a feminine role associated with nurturing, raised anxious questions for boys. Given that the nurturing role in the domestic context is so readily identified with that which is 'good', boys are left unsure as to how to be good yet not be seen to be feminine. The resultant anxiety generated by this for boys is, according to Cohen, resolved in the street gang. Here the assertion of power through physical prowess rather than negotiation, the taking of risks rather than keeping safe, the thrill and excitement of breaking the rules rather than accepting them, all provide not only the avenues and the motivation for delinquent behaviour but also an expression of themselves as young *men*.

Cohen, however, did not really pursue his analysis of delinquency along these lines. He rather presumed that delinquency was primarily a working class phenomenon. So his explanation of delinquent behaviour ultimately downgrades what he has to say about masculinity in favour of upgrading the emphasis on class and class conflict. For Cohen, the delinquent subculture is seen to be a consequence of a working class collective response to the shared experience of being judged by middle class values and the frustration which results from this. This does not mean that Cohen did not recognize other possible motivations for delinquent behaviour; he did. For example, he viewed female delinquency primarily in terms of the expression of deviant sexuality, and he viewed middle class delinquent behaviour primarily in terms of 'drag racing' or 'joy riding' (in the 1950s American sense of the term). This latter type of delinquent behaviour was seen by Cohen as a masculine protest against female authority.

Connell (1987) has pointed out that there are a number of reasons why sex role theory in general constitutes an attractive starting point for explanations concerned with gender and gender difference. He offers us three reasons why this might be the case. First, sex role theory presumes to move us beyond biology as a way of explaining sex differences in behaviour. As an approach it replaces biology with learned social expectations. Second, role theory in general and sex role theory in particular, provides a mechanism whereby an understanding of the impact of social structure can be inserted into an understanding of individual personality. The process of socialization is obviously crucial in this and this facilitates a way of thinking about the contribution played by different kinds of institutions in mediating the effects of structure on individuals. Third, given the emphasis on the socialization process, role theory offers a politics of change. If men and women are what they are because of the oppressive experience and impact of the socialization process, if this process can be changed, so can men and women.

As Connell (1987) argues, these virtues are substantial. There is, however, a central difficulty contained within them. This difficulty has been alluded to already in our discussion of the way in which sex role theory has been applied within criminology; that is, the difficulty highlighted by the fundamental resilience of the biological category of sex. Connell expresses this problem in this way:

> The very terms 'female role' and 'male role', hitching a biological term to a dramaturgical one, suggest what is going on . . . With sex roles, the underlying biological dichotomy seems to have persuaded many theorists that there is no power relationship here at all. The 'female role' and the 'male role' are tacitly treated as equal.
>
> (Connell, 1987: 50–1)

This tacit treatment of the sex roles as if they were equal has the effect of drawing attention away from analysing social reality in terms of power relationships. It also implies a concern with what should be the case as opposed to how people genuinely experience that social reality. In other words, it is a way of thinking about masculinity (and femininity) which cannot capture its fragile tentative, and negotiated character.

So while sex role theory has had some influence on criminological thinking in some attempts to explain the maleness of crime, that influence has been limited not only by the failure of criminology and criminologists to reflect upon its value (the downgrading of gender over class, for example), but also by the limitations inherent within the theoretical framework of sex role theory itself. Such limitations, as highlighted above, point to the need for a theoretical framework which can at least encompass an understanding of the power basis to gender relations. It is in developing an understanding of masculinity in this respect that the influence of both radical and socialist feminism cited earlier can be found.

Categorical theory and criminology

Categorical theory refers to a range of theoretical perspectives, emanating primarily from the feminist movement, which promote an understanding of gender relations by reference to two opposing categories: men and women. As a term it was first used by Connell (1987). Understanding gender relations in these terms identifies both a theory and a politics for action. The categories, men and women, constitute both the units of analysis in which to understand gender relations and the source of explanation for those relations. The key concepts here are patriarchy, domination, oppression and exploitation. Within this conceptual apparatus men are deemed the powerful and women are deemed the other. Under this heading it is possible to group the potential influence of a range of feminist perspectives from radical feminism and socialist feminism to cultural feminism.

In criminology, this kind of categorical analysis has had its most profound effect in the study of sexual violence. The compelling evidence for thinking about sexual violence in terms of power relations, and particularly in terms of the power which men wield over women, has been well argued by radical feminists in particular. The notion that all men keep all women in a state of fear was revolutionary not only in its public, personal and political implications but also in the avenue it provided for recognizing a further dimension to the maleness of the crime problem.

It must be remembered that sexual violence is not exclusively a male activity and neither are all the victims of sexual violence exclusively female. Nevertheless an ungendered understanding of sexual violence would be only a partial one and a criminology which failed to acknowledge the nature and extent of sexual violence would be incomplete. However, an analysis of sexual violence couched in categorical terms is severely limited as a way both of understanding the nature and extent of that violence and as a way of understanding either the expression of masculinity or of femininity. This occurs for two reasons.

First, a concern with the category 'man' produces statements which characterize the behaviour of typical men. In this context this process equates the category 'man' with the potential for sexual violence. Hence the statement, 'All men are potential rapists'. Such a process does a disservice to any individual experience of being male and/or being female. As Connell states, it presents a 'false universalism' which does not resonate with lived social reality. In one sense, then, it could be said that categorical analysis takes us little further, theoretically, than sex role theory.

Second, a focus on the category man equates that category with masculinity. This equation presumes that there is one universal form of masculinity (or, on the other hand, femininity) which is static. In one sense, of course, this tendency towards universalism and quiescence in understanding gender relations present in radical versions of feminism was designed as much to serve political purposes as it was to serve theories of gender relations. However, it is the theoretical implications of these ideas which are of prime concern here.

These limitations taken together should not serve to undermine the profound importance that feminist work, which has been loosely identified here as categorical, has had on our understanding of the nature of gender relations in general and the expression of masculinity in particular. Without this work it would not have been possible for theorists to recognize the need to connect the emphasis on patriarchally rooted power relations with both individually and collectively negotiated identities of masculinity and femininity. But in a sense the question left unanswered by feminist work is the same as that posed by Brittain (1989).

Brittain (1989) identified the problem of trying to understand the relationship between masculinism, the ideology which supports male dominance, and masculinity(ies), the individually negotiated and fragile identities constructed by men. This is the gap left by feminist work in this area which Connell (1987) and Messerschmidt (1993) have attempted to bridge, the latter especially in the particular context of understanding crime.

Doing gender as criminology

In some respects the problem of 'doing gender' is the problem of understanding how any social action is constituted; how to find the balance between the impact of social structure and the choice of social action. In general sociological theory the work of Giddens (1984) has been particularly significant in finding a way to avoid the determinism inherent in a structuralist position on the one hand and the voluntarism inherent in a position which gives primacy to freedom of choice on the other. His work encourages us to think about the ways in which structure is constituted, reconstituted and changed by human actors through their everyday activities. These processes which apply to the general construction of social action also apply to the way in which gender relations are negotiated. The theoretical question to answer, then, to paraphrase Connell (1987), is how is gender organized as an ongoing concern?

Messerschmidt (1993), developing the work of Connell and influenced by Giddens, has offered one way of thinking about how gender is accomplished in the context of criminal behaviour. This analysis endeavours to identify the way in which expression of masculinities constitutes a continuous thread in criminal behaviour from the use of violence in the street through to involvement in 'white collar' crime. He suggests that there are three specific social structures underpinning gender relations from which such a continuity can be derived: the gender division of labour, the gender relations of power, and sexuality. None of these is a constant entity. Their specific form varies through time and space but, taken together, they define the conditions under which gender identities are constructed. In other words, these structures define the conditions under which expressions of masculinity and femininity are constructed. This feature has been defined by Connell (1987) as 'hegemonic masculinity'.

Hegemony is a term borrowed from Gramsci referring to the way in which one class or group can dominate a society by consent. According to Connell (1987) in the expressions of masculinity to be found in late modern societies, hegemonic power is possessed by those males who give expression to normative heterosexuality. This is achieved in the three domains of gender relations identified above in different but related ways. So, for example, it is found in the dominant notion of the male as breadwinner (from the gender division of labour); it is found in the definition of homosexuality but not lesbianism as a crime (from the gender relations of power); and it is found in the objectification of heterosexual women in the media (from the arena of sexuality).

Normative heterosexuality is that form of masculinity which is valued in all aspects of social life (as suggested by the examples offered above) and in being so valued it defines both the structure and the form of the struggle of any individual man to live up to the power of its expectations. At the same time it structures the lives of those who fail, or choose not to engage in such a struggle. As Messerschmidt (1993: 76) states, 'it defines masculinity through difference from, and desire for, women'. It also defines the kinds of possibilities available for variations in masculinity.

So, if this version of masculinity (normative, white, heterosexual masculinity) possesses hegemonic power then it follows that not only does this serve to provide individual men with a sense of themselves as more of a man or less of a man, but also it serves to downgrade other versions of masculinity – homosexuality, for example – as well as downgrading femininity. Normative heterosexuality gives credence to a hierarchical structure which underpins the sense we have of ourselves as gendered subjects while simultaneously permitting an array of expressed masculinities and femininities. Such variations from the normative offer templates for individual action which are differentially valued and differently expressed in relation to normative heterosexuality for both men and women. In this sense, as Messerschmidt (1993: 79) states, 'gender is an accomplishment'; something we are all required to work at, and to provide some account of, in our relationships with others. From this starting point in understanding gender relations, Messerschmidt (1993) goes on to offer one of the most thoroughgoing descriptive accounts of the relationship between masculinities and crime, which we shall discuss briefly here.

> Research reveals that men construct masculinities in accord with their position in social structures and therefore their access to power and resources.
>
> (Messerschmidt, 1993: 119)

This leads Messerschmidt to analyse a variety of social contexts in which differential access to power and resources produces differently emphasized constructions of masculinity. In the context of crime this results in the consideration of three key locations: the street, the workplace and the home. In each of these locations Messerschmidt provides a detailed account of the variety of ways in which masculinity is given expression to, from the pimp on the street to the sharp business practice of the rising white collar executive, to expressions of male proprietory in the form of various violences in the home.

All of these accounts are offered as a means of demonstrating the ways in which men display their manliness to others and to themselves. So while the business executive might use his position and power to sexually harass his female secretary in perhaps more subtle ways than the pimp controls his women, the effects are both the same. In this particular example, the women concerned are subjugated and the men concerned are affirmed as normatively heterosexual men.

Messerschmidt's (1993) work, however, is really at the edge of criminological theorizing and empirical investigation. While some work is ongoing which takes the issue of masculinity as its focal concern for criminological investigation, that work has yet to impact upon mainstream criminological thought. The reasons for this are both to do with the intransigence of the traditional concerns of criminology, on the one hand, and the (potential) inherent limitations of this kind of gendered work on the other. These limitations are twofold in character.

First, while all men might be potential rapists, not all men do rape. Why they choose to rape, or not rape, can be understood only in part by reference to the available, socially acceptable styles of masculine expression. Another part of the explanation for their choice must lie with understanding the contribution of motivations such as desire, pleasure, risk seeking, etc. Raising concepts such as they may, of course, take us down the highly individualistic route of psychoanalysis; but they might also lead us to reconceptualize our understandings of criminality in terms of what Katz (1988) calls *The Seductions of Crime*. As Jefferson (1993) argues, unless we understand the pleasures of crime as well as the opportunities for crime, we shall never really have a complete picture of criminal behaviour.

Second, there is a tendency within some of the literature which centralizes a concern with masculinity to seek to explain all kinds of criminal behaviour by reference to that masculinity, from state terrorism to joy riding. This tendency runs the risk of being tautological and reflects the underpinning desire of many criminologists and criminologies to produce a universal explanation of crime. This desire betrays the discipline's inherent commitment to the modernist as opposed to the postmodernist project and its wish to generate a meaningful policy agenda implied by that commitment.

Summary: gendering the criminal or gendering criminology?

From the thematic overview presented here it is fair to say that in various ways criminology has both implicitly and explicitly addressed the question of sex and crime. In other words, there has been a tradition of work concerned to examine the differences between male and female offending behaviour, their experiences of the criminal justice system, and to invoke the importance of sex as a variable in explaining those differences. Indeed, early feminist work gave significant impetus to studies addressing those concerns. Where there has been less work generated, with the notable exception of the work of Cain, Carlen, Eaton, Worrall and others, has been within a theoretical framework which explicitly deals with the question of gender as it both impacts upon women and men.

Gender has remained implicit to criminology rather than explicitly explored by it. As Jefferson (1993) has argued, the view has been sustained that crime was men's work (and not women's) and that domain criminological assumption has not been adequately explored. This raises the question of not whether the criminal is gendered or not, but the extent to which criminology has, or can be, gendered or not.

Scraton (1990) observes that there is a 'pervasiveness of hegemonic masculinity' within the discipline, 'found covertly in the academic discourses which prevail within malestream criminology'. This statement sensitizes us to understanding the discipline, not just as one peopled and dominated by men, but as one in which in the very fabric of its structure has taken as given views of men, women and crime. This has its origins in what Eagle-Russett (1989) has called the nineteenth century 'sexual science' which laid the foundations for subsequent images of men and women. Those images have, according to Naffine (1987), associated female crime with activities surrounding sexuality and what is considered to be the normal expression of sexuality. They are images which have also most readily associated men with criminal activity:

> Feminist theory is likely to dismantle the long-standing dichotomy of the devilish and daring criminal man and the unappealing inert

conforming woman. The threat it poses to a masculine criminology is therefore considerable.

(Naffine, 1987: 133)

The threat is still there. Criminology has, as yet, done little to dismantle it. So while the criminal and criminal activity may well be gendered, criminology has yet to be.

Conclusion

This chapter has explored the different ways in which assumptions concerning the concept of gender have been more or less hidden within the criminological enterprise. Criminology, of course, has no special status in the way in which it has rendered questions of gender invisible. Such invisibility is, arguably, deeply rooted in conceptions of what counts as knowledge and who can know things to which all the social (and natural) sciences have been subjected (Harding, 1991). The question remains, however, as to how much there is to be learned about crime, its causation, and the processes of criminalization, by rendering questions of gender more explicit.

It is clear that much has been learned concerning the locus of criminal behaviour, how it is manifested, and by whom from that feminist work which has exposed the nature and extent of broadly defined sexual violence against women and children. It is also clear that recasting an understanding of that kind of criminal behaviour in terms of masculinity has provided an increasingly perceptive insight into some aspects of its underlying 'causal' processes. (See for example the work of Scully, 1990, on convicted rapists.) The question remains, however, the inherent hegemonic masculinity of the discipline notwithstanding, as to how and under what circumstances gender is the prevailing or key explanatory variable. Put more simply, is the opportunist burglar expressing his manhood or something else? As I have stated elsewhere

A gendered lens certainly helps us see some features of the crime problem more clearly perhaps; but under what circumstances is that clarity made brighter by gender or distorted by it.

(Walklate, 1995: 192)

If mainstream (malestream) criminology is to be persuaded to meet the challenge which much of this work on gender constitutes for it, then that work itself needs to consider its own assumptions in a reflexive and self-critical manner.

As was demonstrated within the critical evaluation offered of left realism, it is simply not enough to assert that questions of gender have been embraced, or that it is through a gendered lens that a solution to the causation of crime may be found. These assertions do not in and of themselves equip us with the understanding of what underpins the circumstances in which gender matters more than any other variable and those circumstances in which it does not. What may be the incontrovertible outcome of taking gender seriously, however, is the recognition that the answer to that process may be found only outside the conventional criminological domain, issues which will be differently addressed in Chapters 6 and 7.

Further reading

One way of mapping the changing nature of the way in which questions of gender have been addressed or not addressed within criminology would be to compare and contrast Heidensohn (1985) *Women and Crime* with Walklate (1995) *Gender and Crime*, each provides a usefully different overview of the kinds of gendered questions criminology might address. A good feel for the variety of work emanating from feminist work relevant to criminology is offered in Gelsthorpe and Morris (eds) (1990) *Feminist Perspectives in Criminology*. Those wishing to explore in greater detail an understanding of the relationship between masculinity and crime will find Messerschmidt (1993) *Masculinities and Crime* invaluable.

Crime, politics and welfare

So far this text has evidenced some of the key theoretical developments which have occurred within criminology since the mid-1970s. In the course of reviewing those theoretical strands it has been shown that it is possible to forge different links between them and the world of politics. In other words, as theories, they may lend themselves to different uses and interpretations by those occupying the political domain. The question remains, however, as to what kind of relationship might exist between that which has occurred within the political domain and the formation of an agenda for criminology. In this chapter, then, we shall be concerned to contextualize the possibilities for a criminological agenda by mapping the interconnections between criminology, criminal justice and social justice: but why make these connections?

Principles of social justice are fundamental to the organization of any society. An appreciation of the way in which any particular society believes that the rewards and punishments in that society should be distributed reveals much about the fundamental (taken for granted) features of that society. Moreover there are different ways in which such an appreciation might be developed. In this chapter, in order to engage in an analysis of this kind we shall address the issue of social justice through three interlinked issues: an analysis of the changing nature of what has been understood as the 'welfare state' from 1945 to 1995; the ways in which that changing conception of welfare might facilitate an understanding of the criminalization process; and the outcome of that process for questions relating to gender, the family, the idea of the underclass and crime. However, it is to a consideration of the changing nature of the 'welfare state' that we shall turn first of all.

Understanding the welfare state

As has already been indicated, the way in which any society organizes its social policies presupposes some notion of how it is felt that the rewards and punishments in that society are to be distributed. In the UK political views concerning the appropriateness of the distribution of such rewards and punishments have changed in emphasis, arguably, over a remarkably short period of time. That change has been encapsulated, some would say, in the customerization of citizenship (Edgar, 1991). Whatever terms are used to articulate the way in which the distributive process works, the principles on which the process works are underpinned by the notions of needs, rights and social justice and the role that the state might play in meeting these for its citizens.

Analytically speaking there are different ways in which needs, rights and justice might be intermeshed which reflect different ideas of appropriate political and social organization (liberal democracy as compared with state socialism, for example, see George and Wilding, 1976). Indeed, as many of the societies which once comprised 'eastern Europe' moved from state socialism towards a more democratic form of political organization, it was these very issues which those societies grappled with in a very real sense. For many of those societies it was within this movement in which the role of the state was subject to its most critical exposure. Indeed, in any society it is a moot point whether or not it is the welfare of the individual which is at stake in the distribution of the rewards and punishments or the welfare of the state (see Offe, 1984). In this particular context, understanding the potential for the formulation of a criminological agenda it will be of value to reflect upon how the notions of needs, rights and justice have been joined together in the UK during the period 1945 to 1995.

Citizen and state in the 1950s

The Beveridge reforms, implemented in the few years immediately after the Second World War, were intended to provide protection against the five great social ills: disease, squalor, ignorance, idleness and want. Those reforms (according to Marshall, 1981) while embedded in and arguably consolidating earlier social policy legislation, marked a development in extending the nature of citizenship. That extension moved the rights of the citizen from the realm of the civil and political into the realm of the social. In other words, it was considered appropriate that being a full member of society consisted of the right to share in the life of a civilized human being according to the standards currently prevailing in that society.

The key to the extension of citizenship into this social realm was the introduction of an insurance based benefits system. This, it was argued, constituted a clear extension of such social rights since by implication this system put into practice the idea of a contract between the individual (citizen) and the state. Put simply, if as an individual citizen you paid into the system, the state offered you some guarantees in return.

This contractual basis to the post Second World War reforms, however, did not extend to every citizen automatically. It always contained within it a notion of less eligibility. In other words, if individuals did not pay into the system they were less eligible for rewards from it. In practical terms this meant being subjected to a system of means testing. So, arguably the Beveridge proposals always excluded those who were seen to be 'undeserving'. In some respects, therefore, this legislative package built upon and consolidated the historical distinction which had always been made between the 'deserving' and the 'undeserving' poor, a distinction which threads its way through not only the social security legislation but also thinking within the criminal justice system. This latter effect is best illustrated in the underlying philosophy of the Criminal Injuries Compensation Board.

It has been argued that the formation of the Criminal Injuries Compensation Board constituted the last brick of the welfare state to be cemented with the post Second World War principles of Beveridge (Mawby and Walklate, 1994). It was the groundwork of Margery Fry, a key criminal justice campaigner of the 1950s, which largely influenced its formation in 1964. Fry's argument was constructed in this way: as all taxpayers could be potential victims of violent crime, and since the state forbade its citizens to arm themselves as a means of protection against violent crime, when individual citizens became victims of violent crime, and it could be demonstrated that they were the innocent party, the state should assume some responsibility for having failed to protect them. Within this argument, then, which informed the foundation of the Criminal Injuries Compensation Board, it is possible to identify two key principles of the welfare state: the contractual obligation between the citizen and the state, and the notion of less eligibility.

This way of thinking about the relationship between the citizen and the state lasted until the 1970s. It was a view in which the citizen had social rights and the state had obligations to fulfil those rights provided that the contract between the citizen and the state had been fulfilled; in other words, provided that those rights were deserved. So, arguably, even within the

Beveridge ideal not everyone was included as full social citizens: the unde-serving were always excluded from full social citizenship. What lies beneath the recognition of this is the continuous thread of presumptions between the 1950s and the 1990s concerning the issue of social justice. In understanding this thread it is possible to understand how it was that a change of empha-sis in the relationship between the citizen and the state took place.

To summarize: while the notion that the 1950s represented a period of political and social consensus is somewhat problematic, it is clear that the Macmillan adage of 'You've never had it so good' conveyed a powerful sym-bolic message at a time when the end of rationing, the extension of edu-cational opportunities, the building of council houses, and for the most part near full employment, became significant and taken for granted features of people's everyday lives. Crime itself, the caveats concerning the use of official statistics as reliable indicators of crime rates notwithstanding, had declined from a post-war peak by 1955 (Wootton, 1959). Although recorded crime began to rise sharply again at the end of the decade, especially violent crime (Morris, 1989; Rock, 1990), with adolescents being increasingly identified as 'trouble'. Arguably, however, it really was not until the early 1970s that this sense of general comfort, associated with the 1950s (with some underlying tensions evident in relation to young people), began to be undermined.

Citizen and state in the 1990s

The Labour government of the early 1970s presided over high rates of inflation which set the economic framework in which changes in public policy were likely to take place. Moreover, by the time the international recession of the mid-1970s began to take effect, the scene was set for a change in political climate as well as a consequent change in social policy and what was considered to be the appropriate relationship between the citi-zen and the state. Public expenditure was seen to be at the heart of the econ-omic difficulties being experienced and the plan for reducing the rate of inflation by restoring incentives included removing what Margaret Thatcher referred to as the 'nanny state'. In 1977, she wrote:

> The sense of being self reliant, of playing a role within the family, of owning one's property, of paying one's way, are all part of the spiritual ballast which maintains responsible citizenship and a solid foundation from which people look around to see what more they can do for others and themselves.
>
> (Thatcher, 1977: 97)

In this statement lies the embryo of political ideas which were to change the direction of the relationship between the citizen and the state throughout the

1980s and early 1990s, changes which were also fuelled by the civil disturbances of 1981. Those disturbances, while varied in their cause, marked the beginning of a decade in which the legitimacy which the criminal justice system formerly presumed it possessed was seriously tested. Indeed, it was within the criminal justice system, as well as in other areas of public policy, in which the relationship between the citizen and state was given new expression.

Put simply, the change in direction in the relationship between the citizen and the state was primarily about reducing the obligations of the state to provide and increasing the obligations (as opposed to the rights) of the citizen to contribute to society and provide for themselves. Such a view was constituted within an overarching belief that giving a simultaneous free reign to market forces would increase competition, expand consumer choice and provide a way out of economic difficulties. For the individual, these expectations were encapsulated by 'active citizenship'. As Douglas Hurd (the then Home Secretary) stated in 1989:

> The idea of active citizenship is a necessary complement to that of the
> enterprise culture. Public Service may once have been the duty of an elite
> but today it is the responsibility of all who have time or money to spare.
>
> (Hurd, 1989)

In other words individual citizens no longer fulfilled their obligations to the state through the payment of their taxes or national insurance contributions. In these particular economic circumstances the welfare of the state, as opposed to the welfare of the individual, demanded more of them. In this case, the individual subjects of Hurd's 'active citizenship' are the successful, enterprising, consuming, property owning classes (the deserving) not those living on state benefits (the undeserving).

Again this view of citizenship, while evidenced in a range of policy initiatives, was clearly present within the world of the criminal justice system. Perhaps found in its most definitive form in the massive growth of Neighbourhood Watch Schemes (in which 'good' citizens become the 'eyes and ears' of the police), the growth of Victim Support as a voluntary organization, the increasing importance of the symbolism of the victim politically, and the generation of consumer charters and concerns with consumer satisfaction within policing. In all of these developments, the poor in general are those most likely to be the objects of this active citizenship rather than its subjects simply because they do not possess the power to pay or make their claims count. Some would say a rearticulation of the principle of less eligibility. Others would say that principle never disappeared.

The picture of this changing emphasis in citizen–state relationships is undoubtedly more complex than has been outlined here. It has been presented here as though it was a process which sustained historical divisions in a uniform fashion. However, as Lister has stated:

The extent to which women and black people have always been the victims of exclusionary practices is all too often ignored by those who deplore today's retreat from supposedly universal rights. The point being that universal rights never existed in the first place.

(Lister, 1990: 27)

The rationale for such a view can be found in the extent to which in the formulation of the legislation of the late 1940s there are presumptions (understandable given the cultural and political norms of the time) concerning race and gender which have not been spelt out here. The Beveridge proposals worked with a notion of female dependency on a male breadwinner who was also implicitly white. Presumptions such as these, of course (then as now), were always overlaid by issues of class and poverty.

Morris (1994), for example, has argued there is a strong historical continuity in those who find themselves defined as part of the 'dangerous classes'. In comparing Victorian England with the 1990s, she states:

Dependency, then, as now, is largely explained as a defect of character, though there is also a fear that adequate provision for the poor could undermine the work incentive among lower paid workers. Even Marx, who saw poverty as an inevitable product of capitalism, with the poor as its helpless victims, identifies a depraved and decadent 'social scum'.

(Morris, 1994: 157)

Part of that historical continuity has also undoubtedly been the extent to which claimants on the state have never been free from moral condemnation and stigmatization, and in this respect have always constituted part of that group excluded from full social citizenship from 1945 to the present day. The question remains, why should an understanding of this relationship between the citizen and the state be of importance for criminology?

Why is it important to understand the relationship between the citizen and the state?

A key question underpins the discussion so far: how much responsibility should we assume, collectively, for the most vulnerable in our society, however we might choose to define the nature of that vulnerability? As this discussion has highlighted so far, the answer to this question of the just distribution of rewards and punishments is linked with the question of citizenship: who is included and excluded in the relationship between the citizen and the state? It has also been suggested that, while that relationship has changed in emphasis between 1945 and 1995, there are strong historical continuities underpinning the mechanisms of social exclusion in particular. Those mechanisms of social exclusion have been differently identified as the distinction between the deserving and the undeserving, the principle of less eligibility, or the notion of the 'dangerous classes'. This last label provides the clearest clue to the importance of understanding these processes for criminology. The 'dangerous classes' provide the criminal justice system with much of its work. How they are variously and differently criminalized, and the changing social processes which feed that process of criminalization constitute the stuff of criminology. There is, however, one crucial issue still to be addressed in understanding the potential impact of these social processes between 1945 and 1995 before the nature of that criminological agenda is unfolded in more detail.

One of the most striking features of the period 1979 to 1995 has been the overwhelming increase in the gap between the rich and the poor (Scott, 1994; Hutton, 1995). This has led Hutton (1995) in particular to talk of the 30/30/40 society, emphasizing not only the gap between those securely well off and those not but also the increasing number of people who are economically vulnerable. The impact of that increasing economic vulnerability for an increasing number of people has been nowhere less felt than in the criminal justice system. As Carlen states:

> The striking increase in inequality and wealth which has been a major feature of the last decade has been accompanied by a steady increase in the prison population . . . This is not surprising. Whatever else prisons may be for, they have always housed large numbers of the poor, the unemployed, the unemployable, the homeless, the physically ill, and the mentally disturbed.
>
> (Carlen, 1988: 8)

In other words, there is a relationship between the changing size in the ranks of the 'dangerous classes' and the levels of work likely to be facing the criminal justice agencies. While the nature of this relationship has been hugely contested (and denied) politically, it nevertheless points up the interconnections between the distribution of social justice and the likelihood of being subjected to the criminal justice system.

This relationship also points to another problematic issue. If those people who come before the criminal justice system are increasingly likely to be the kinds of people identified above, then how might such people be treated justly within and by the criminal justice system? What is a socially just punishment for mentally disturbed offenders who find themselves homeless following the implementation of policies designed to provide care in the community? Asking questions of this kind clearly conveys the very real way in which social justice and criminal justice are interrelated.

To summarize: a criminology concerned with questions such as these offers an agenda which neither subjugates its work to the vagaries of politics nor consigns its explanations to the realm of individual responsibility, both of which have been evidenced in earlier chapters. This kind of criminological agenda has as one of its central concerns the processes of criminalization, not just of individuals but social groups, alongside an understanding of how those processes are structurally informed. For the left idealist (see Chapter 2) defining a criminological agenda in this way would be seriously limited by the lack of attention it would pay, by implication, to the crimes of the powerful; those who rarely have to face the attention of the criminal justice agencies. The fact that such attention is missing for so much crime which costs, however, asserts all the more the need for a careful understanding of what underpins the processes for those who are in receipt of such attention. Arguably it is only from a position which has such a relatively clear vision on the interconnections between criminal justice and social justice that the greater injustices of the activities of the relatively powerful can be most effectively exposed.

In order to develop such criminological concerns in greater detail, the rest of this chapter, then, will take as its substantive examples two areas in which such interconnections can be made: the relationship between gender, crime and poverty, and the relationship between the family, class and crime. We shall consider each of these areas in turn.

Gender, crime, and poverty

As was observed in the foregoing discussion, the kinds of social policies any society puts into place articulate a view of what people's entitlements from the state might look like. Historically, those entitlements have been distributed in a gender blind fashion. For example, the Beveridge proposals were rooted in what might be termed 'natural' images of femininity largely emanating from the earlier legislative reforms concerned in a variety of ways with 'educating the mother' (Lewis, 1980). This was translated into what has been called the 'ideology of female dependency' crystallized in the principle of insurance. This assumed that all workers were by definition male with married women being insured through their husband's contributions. Moreover, if a husband left the marriage he did so with his insurance records intact; if the wife left she did so for the means tested National Assistance Board. While there have been significant specific policy changes since the Beveridge proposals, little has changed this basic ideological relationship between the state and women and their claim for state support. The more a (female) claimant deviates from the ideology of the dependent female the more difficult is made her claim for support. It has been argued that this ideological position is exacerbated when the question of who comprises the poor is examined more closely.

Historically women have always been among the poorest in society (see, for example, Booth, 1895). However, in the early 1980s an added twist was given to the debate concerning the rising number of poor people in the development of what was called the 'feminization of poverty' thesis. This thesis suggested that significant shifts were occurring in the population comprising 'the poor'. Women in particular, it was argued, were increasingly likely to find themselves living in poverty. A number of reasons were suggested for this: women were living longer and were thus likely to constitute a higher proportion of poor elderly people; changes in social policy were resulting in more women finding themselves with dependent relatives to care for supported only through the benefits system; more young women were choosing to have children on their own placing them within the benefit system; and as the gap between rich and poor expanded more women were likely to find themselves living in families on low incomes. The resultant effect of these factors, combined with the sex segregated nature of the labour market, its inherent sexism, alongside the ideological claiming relationship women have with the state, determined that women's chances of finding themselves in poverty increased. The question remains, however, on the extent to which a gendered process such as this one, reflecting as it does a highly gendered notion of social justice connects with the process of criminalization.

'Women offer sex for sale as slump hits the valleys' ran a headline in *The Independent on Sunday* on 15 September 1991 portraying one view of the interconnections between changing socio-economic circumstances and the way in which those circumstances might push some women towards lawbreaking behaviour. Indeed, historically, prostitution has been one way to supplement meagre incomes for women. There are others. Cook (1989) argues that fiddling the benefit system is one kind of lawbreaking behaviour committed by women which is increasingly seen as a rational response to being in poverty and on benefit. Of course, what Cook goes on to document is how much more effectively this kind of lawbreaking behaviour is policed than that associated with tax evasion, for example.

Prostitution and defrauding the benefit system are, arguably, less serious crimes. Carlen's (1988) study offers a life history account of the criminal careers of thirty-nine of the more serious kind of lawbreaking women in which four factors were identified as constituting turning points in these women's criminal careers: being in residential care, having a drug or alcohol addiction, the desire for excitement, and being in poverty.

Here then there is some evidence that there are interconnections between the gendered inequalities generated by social policies playing themselves out in the processes of criminalization. Yet it must be remembered that women's tendency to engage in criminal behaviour (as recorded by official statistics), their increasing poverty notwithstanding, still occurs at a far less rate than men's despite them being subjected to the greater policing and surveillance associated with living on benefit.

Over a million women head one-parent families and the majority of them live not only in poverty but also in fear – that due to official inefficiency the supplementary benefit cheque won't arrive; that the benefit will be withdrawn while their circumstances are reviewed; that they will be accused of any of a number of fraudulent practices relating to the claiming of supplementary benefit; that they are under constant surveillance, from both neighbours and officials watching to catch them out if they appear to be sharing household expenses with anyone else; that their children will be taken into residential care if they themselves finally crack under the strain of bringing up kids in poverty.

(Carlen, 1988: 2)

Under these circumstances it is all the more surprising that more women do not find themselves choosing lawbreaking behaviour as a way of managing difficult circumstances. There are potentially a number of different explanations which could be proffered as a way of understanding the changes that these processes imply, one of which might be to reconsider the accuracy of the 'feminization of poverty' thesis. Gimenez (1990) attempts to do this.

Gimenez offered an historical analysis of the changing composition of the poor in the United States from 1966 to 1984. From these data she concluded that the proportion of poor men grew at a faster rate than the proportion of poor women over this time period and rather than this being particularly problematic for women it was particularly problematic for young men. In other words, while women do constitute a significant proportion of those finding themselves in poverty, the general trends being observed in relation to the poor could be just as adequately explained in terms of the broader imiseration of the working class as much as being the particular feminization of poverty. As Hutton (1994: 23) has observed in the UK, 'single parents, the young unemployed, and families living on income support are propelling the growth of poverty', in the general circumstances in which the gap between rich and poor appears to be ever widening. In other words there is no reason to presume that conditions for women are worsening at a rate any greater than those for other groups of people who find themselves poor.

A similar set of circumstances may be prevailing in the UK as in the United States, given Campbell's (1993) analysis of the civil disturbances of 1991. Given those disturbances, there is some reason to believe that the worsening economic conditions for those excluded from full social citizenship are taking a particular toll on the young, especially young men. The responses that young men and young women are constructing to those worsening conditions may, of course, be different, and those differences may be constructed in a highly gendered way. However, the discussion offered here, by implication, leads to a consideration of the way in which those gendered responses are preconditioned by the changing relationship between citizen and state in changing socio-economic circumstances. They may also be overlaid by questions relating to social class, as the discussion below will illustrate.

It may be then, that the relationship between women, crime and poverty, and men, crime and poverty may be very similar. As Box (1987) has argued, this is not to offer an excuse for criminal behaviour but merely to understand that the kinds of choices people may make are not in circumstances of their own choosing. These changing economic and political circumstances do not only impinge themselves upon the poor. As Hutton's (1995) analysis readily admits, 40 per cent of the UK population have fared rather well in more general worsening economic circumstances. Moreover, as we move towards the end of the millennium, British women will constitute an increasingly higher proportion of those adults comprising the full time working population. Given that being in work offers at least as many (if not more) opportunities for lawbreaking behaviour, a key issue for the criminological agenda might be to consider the relationship between the changing nature of the labour market and the propensity (of women) to engage in crime.

The last question notwithstanding, in policy terms it is evident that the groups identified by Hutton (1994) are those same groups for whom access to social security benefits has become increasingly difficult since 1979. The appropriateness or otherwise of these moves is not the issue for discussion here. What is appropriate, however, is the ways in which the targeting of groups of this kind has become politically both implicitly and explicitly connected with the question of crime. Not necessarily through the concept of gender, as the discussion above has been concerned with, but by highlighting the changing nature of the family as the key causal mechanism in which to locate an understanding of both social and criminological problems.

Conceptions of the family, the underclass, and crime

The role given to the nature and impact of family life as a contributory factor in law breaking behaviour has varied in the course of criminological history. Early sociologically influenced studies of crime paid particular attention to factors such as family tension, the 'broken' home, patterns of discipline in the family, neglect, and criminality within the family, as possible indicators of, and explanations for, especially juvenile delinquency. However, as with other areas of investigation, focusing on the family in this way has been more or less fashionable at different historical points in time with the available empirical evidence being used in various ways at those different historical moments.

Arguably, any debate concerning the family is always tinged with political interest, since such debate is also always embedded in some notion of what counts as 'normal' family life. As Stone's (1995) historical analysis of divorce serves to remind us, families in earlier centuries were often not the 'ideal types' politicians would wish us to believe they were, being frequently 'broken' by death in childbirth, absent fathers, much reduced life expectancy and so on. Nevertheless, during the 1990s in particular, the public political debate on both the nature of crime and lawbreaking behaviour, centred the role of the family. In this chapter, then, we shall consider the criminological evidence on the role of the family as a contributory factor in lawbreaking behaviour, the differing political interpretations which have been placed on that evidence, and the policy implications which flow from those interpretations. In so doing we shall pay particular attention to the ideological assumptions underpinning the images of family life which have become embedded in this debate. But first, why is the family important?

Why is understanding the family important?

While family structures have changed considerably historically, the importance given to the role of the family in criminological research has varied. As was suggested earlier, influenced by sociology, criminological work which has considered the role of the family in contributing to lawbreaking behaviour can be summarized under four main headings: the influence of the 'broken' family, family tension, the quality of parenting, and the 'abusive' family. Much of the work concerned with each of these factors has focused primarily on their relevance for understanding juvenile delinquency and the way in which that concern has manifested itself has varied.

For example, in the years after the Second World War up to the 1960s, a popular thesis connecting family life with juvenile delinquency was to be found in the work of Bowlby (1965). Sponsored by the World Heath Organization, Bowlby's work was initially concerned to address the effects on children of evacuation during the wartime years. His findings, however, while highlighting a number of different circumstances in which parental loss and/or separation resulted in behavioural and/or psychological problems for the children concerned, have been most remembered for the introduction of the notion of 'maternal deprivation'.

One of the factors identified by Bowlby as contributing to behavioural problems (including delinquency) in children was the deprivation of the mother or mother figure in the early years of life especially before the age of 5. In political and social policy terms this was interpreted as meaning that in order to rear problem free children it was necessary for the mother to stay at home. For many families, of course, economic reality dictated that the woman of the house worked (at least on a part-time basis) as often as the man did. However this notion of maternal deprivation served to fuel ideological beliefs about the role of women and their role in the family, beliefs which Wilson (1983) argued contributed to the 'Observer Wife' syndrome and helped sow the seeds of support for the feminist movement of the 1960s. It was, of course, out of that movement that a very different image of the family life of women and children was brought to the surface.

Recasting the family in terms of power relations between men and women led much feminist work to consider the ways in which those power relationships manifest themselves. It is from this work that one notion of the abusive family can be constructed. Understanding the private domain as one in which much criminal activity can occur in the form of rape and violence, certainly both broadened and deepened the criminological agenda, though it was not (and is not) an image of family life which is much in evidence in political rhetoric.

Despite the evidence emanating from the feminist movement that the intact family might constitute just as much of a breeding ground for criminal behaviour as the maternally deprived family it is not difficult to see why concern with the notion of the 'broken family' would lend itself more readily to political use. Whether or not this constitutes a valid interpretation of Bowlby's work in particular, or of work which followed in this vein in general, is however, a moot point. As Currie states:

> The belief that the 'brokenness' of the home itself is of crucial importance in creating delinquency derives mainly from a tradition of studies of the supposed pernicious effects of 'father absence' or of 'maternal deprivation' on the growing child, especially at very early ages. But it has not held up well under the lens of careful research . . . This isn't to say that family disruption is a benign or neutral event in the lives of children; it usually isn't, and many studies show that it can be damaging, at least in the short run – and for some children in the long run as well. But as a precursor of delinquency and other developmental problems, it is overshadowed by the effects of family conflict.
>
> (Currie, 1985: 195–6)

The general empirical findings appear to support Currie's (1985) interpretation of the data. In other words, it is the presence and/or absence of family discord which has been found consistently to be associated with delinquency rather than the absence or presence of a mother or father. Other factors have also been found to be relevant, like, for example, the changing material conditions of the child and the quality of the parenting. What is interesting, at a political level, is that despite the empirical evidence, the importance of the intact nuclear family was given unprecedented weight during the 1980s and 1990s especially in the call for a return to 'family values' or alternatively 'back to basics'. This was a political focus which particularly centred on those at the lower end of the social hierarchy, and perhaps could be most readily identified as the importance of the 'absent father'.

One particular version of the 'absent father' gained especial political prominence in the late 1980s and early 1990s. That version focused on the notion of 'families without fathers' and the possible connections which could be made between rising rates of illegitimacy and rising crime rates. This version of centring the importance of the nuclear family not only neglects to address that version of family life proffered by the feminist movement but also fails to consider the way in which the presence of a father, particularly one with a criminal record, might produce equally problematic effects for the child.

Moreover, the concern to consider the relationship between illegitimacy and rising crime arose from a wider debate which focused on the question of whether or not there was an 'underclass' in Britain. This debate had a number of different strands within it, for example, what were the defining characteristics of the underclass, who comprised the underclass, how big was it, and so on. Indeed, it will be of value to appreciate some of the features of this wider debate in order to understand both how the form and the impact of this particular concern with the family was generated.

The underclass and crime

As this chapter has already highlighted, distinctions have always been made historically between the deserving and undeserving poor, that is, between those who were genuinely poor and those who brought poverty upon themselves. Such distinctions have always carried with them a certain amount of value judgement and social stigma. Historically too there have always been lawbreaking means through which people dealt with their poverty. Indeed, in Marx's discussion of the lumpenproletariat, he used quite pejorative terms with which to describe the 'social scum' of the criminal underclass. More recent debate around the underclass has been little different in both the kinds of analytical distinctions theorists have endeavoured to make in identifying the underclass and the value judgements which have accrued to those so stigmatized, as illustrated below. An attempt will be made here to separate these issues and to consider, primarily, the relevance of this debate in talking about crime.

Recent sociological debate on the underclass has been characterized by three main questions: is the underclass under/below or outside the other social classes? Is it characterized by structural conditions or socio-cultural attitudes? If it exists, how big is it and who constitutes it? We shall address some features of each of these questions in turn.

Runciman (1990) locates the underclass as the seventh social class. He argues that

> the term must be understood to stand not for a group or category of workers systematically disadvantaged in the labour market . . . but for those members of British society whose roles place them more or less permanently at the economic level where benefits are paid by the state to those unable to participate in the labour market at all . . . like the upper class they need to be distinguished as such in institutional, not

statistical, terms, and it is because they can that they constitute the seventh of the seven classes which there are in contemporary Britain.

(Runciman, 1990: 388)

Smith (1992) interprets this definition as meaning that it is possible to identify some sort of minimum standard criterion by which to measure the nature and extent of the underclass, accepting, of course, that this definition constitutes the underclass as a class below the other social classes. Dahrendorf takes a different view:

> The key point in theoretical terms about the underclass seems to me to be that it is precisely not a class. Classes are essentially necessary social forces. It is no accident that Marx tried to link classes, not just to relations but to forces of production; he saw classes as being based on certain central social needs, one class which presides over the existing values and laws and rules and mode of production and the other class which represents some new opportunity for the future some chance of development. The whole point about the underclass of category of those who have dropped through the net is that they are not needed in this sense.
>
> (Dahrendorf, 1992: 57)

Here Dahrendorf is in some respects taking a strictly Marxist definition of class. This would define the underclass as being outside the class system since it has no essential relationship to the means of production. Dahrendorf's concern with the underclass has another aspect to it, however.

For Dahrendorf (following Marshall), the more recent emergence of an underclass is intimately connected with the erosion of social citizenship consequent to the contractions which have taken place within the welfare state. These contractions deny sections of the population access to full social participation in society (as being different from their access to political or legal participation) and result in a process of social segmentation which further militates against full inclusion in society. So as Dahrendorf argues,

> The underclass is the group which combines desolate living conditions and lack of traditional bonds even of class with low skill and hopeless employment prospects. The result is cynicism towards the official values of society bent on work and order. The underclass is not a revolutionary force, but one which will make its presence felt by crime, riots, and also by forming a volatile reserve army of militancy on either extreme of the political spectrum.
>
> (Dahrendorf, The Times, July 1985)

To summarize: Runciman (1990) is suggesting that the underclass forms a class which is below all the other social classes and can be structurally identified as such. Dahrendorf is suggesting that the underclass is outside the class system, and moreover is suggesting that members of the underclass can also be identified by their attitudes. The question is whether or not structural location produces the attitudes or the attitudes result in the structural location. The way in which this question has been debated provides our first glimpse of the way in which the question of the role of the family has been connected to this debate and its relationship with crime. The ideas of Murray (1990) have been particularly influential in this respect.

Murray defines the underclass not just by economic position but also by behaviour:

> When I've used the term underclass I am indeed focusing on a certain type of poor person defined not by his condition e.g. long term unemployed, but by his deplorable behaviour in response to that condition.
>
> (Murray, 1990: 68)

For Murray (1990) there are three predictors of membership of the underclass: illegitimacy, crime, and labour market behaviour. Murray takes illegitimacy to mean two things. First, when a child grows up without two parents from the moment it is born. Second, when illegitimacy is associated with a particular set of attitudes to marriage, i.e. that marriage is not important and has no value. Murray's argument is that this 'pure form' of illegitimacy is rising, especially in the lower social classes, and in those communities where fathers are absent, the children run wild.

Murray's second predictor of membership of the underclass is crime. Again Murray's argument is that crime is rising rapidly: he cites evidence to show that England has a higher burglary rate and car crime rate than the United States, and argues that the rise in violent crime in particular (though lower in England than in the United States) reflects one measure of the development of the underclass. Habitual criminals are by definition members of the underclass and in areas inhabited by habitual criminals alongside the general rising crime rate both fragments those communities and disrupts the norms of socialization. The final definitive indicator of the underclass is reflected in labour market behaviour. This is not simply a measure of unemployment, though that status is obviously a key factor, but it is defined in relation to the number of healthy young males on low incomes who refuse to take jobs.

So for Murray the presence of an underclass is defined by the rate of 'pure' illegitimacy, the level of crime, and the attitude of young males to work:

> when large numbers of young men don't work, the communities around them break down, just as they break down when large numbers of young unmarried women have babies ... Men who do not support families find other ways to prove that they are men, which tend to take various destructive forms.
>
> (Murray, 1990: 22)

The publication of Murray's ideas on the underclass in the *Sunday Times*, ideas which had been very influential in the United States where the issue of race features far more prominently as a defining factor of the underclass, provoked a huge debate.

That debate was largely an empirical one. Were the figures that Murray used to support his argument (that there was an underclass in the UK) correct? Was there any evidence to support the assertions that Murray was making about the key features of that underclass? For example a number of specific questions have been explored: do the underclass have different attitudes to family life, etc. than other social groups (Heath, 1992)? What does the status of illegitimacy and lone parenthood look like (Brown, 1990)? What does the status and availability of work for young males look like and do they or do they not comprise a dependency culture or engage in fraudulent activities (Morris, 1994)? Are these the defining characteristics of the underclass at all (Field, 1990)?

The answers to these questions need not concern us here. What is of interest is the connections to be made between Murray's assertions on illegitimacy, what that consequently implies in relation to family structure and the way in which this is presumed to feed the potential destructiveness of the behaviour of young males. These assertions connect particularly well with the writings of Dennis (1993) and Dennis and Erdos (1992). It is to a discussion of those ideas which we shall now turn.

Dennis and Erdos (1992) locate their concern with what they call the 'dismembered family' within a need to understand and explain the rising crime rate since the 1950s. They argue that intellectuals have denied the importance of understanding what that rising crime rate represents and what underpins it. In their view, in order to understand what those crime figures represent it is important to understand other changes in social relationships occurring at the same time, especially within the family. They accept the view that crime is an activity overwhelmingly engaged in by young men but their argument is that this is largely the result of the way in which child rearing practices have moved outside of 'normal' family structures. This is evidenced in a number of ways.

First, by the increase in the number of divorces. Dennis and Erdos argue that there is now much more increased freedom for fathers to leave their spouse or their children than there was in the 1950s. More liberal divorce laws now mean that, according to their figures, England and Wales has the highest rate of divorce in Europe. Second, at the same time there has been a significant increase in the freedom to cohabit. Cohabitation, they argue, is much more likely to lead to lone parenthood. In 1991, for example, they cite the statistic that 30 per cent of births were outside of marriage. Within this growing number of births outside marriage there has been an especially significant increase in the number of babies born to teenage girls.

These two factors, they argue, separate the act of impregnation from pregnancy. In other words, they are changes which permit young men to escape the consequences of their acts. They are also changes which have two separate effects: a significant number of young males are growing up in families without fathers, and at the same time they are not experiencing any training in fatherhood nor any obligation to act as fathers. The outcome of these effects is increasing crime, echoing Murray's assertion that children in female headed single parent households run wild.

This line of argument melded particularly well with the debate occurring in the political arena. They were ideas which matched especially with a government already committed to a reassertion of family values. Fuelled by the civil disturbances of 1991 which foregrounded the behaviour of white, young men living on council estates as a key social problem, the targeting of families without fathers in social policy terms proceeded relatively unabated, a concern which was given added impetus with the murder of James Bulger in Merseyside in 1992.

The public focus on the disintegration of the nuclear family lent weight to the arguments of a government who had consistently denied that unemployment was connected with rising crime. For here was a view, rooted in a particular reading of the empirical evidence, which gave legitimacy to the already well asserted political view that it was not unemployment or poor social conditions which resulted in a rising crime rate, but the changing nature of family structure and family life. Indeed, this view gathered such political momentum, that in 1993 the Institute for Public Policy Research (IPPR) organized a national conference on 'Families, Children and Crime'. We shall consider some of the key themes raised by that conference on the connections between families and crime before offering some critical assessment of the contribution that focusing on the family in this way can achieve.

It is possible to identify two thematic ways in which the IPPR conference addressed this question of the relationship between the criminal behaviour of young males and crime. The first was to challenge the conceptualization of, and evidence for, both the changing nature of family structure and its impact as presented by Dennis and Erdos. This theme endeavoured, on the one hand, to contextualize the evidence for the rising crime rate by considering other contributory factors to changes in officially recorded crime figures; on the other hand, it was concerned to reinterpret the conditions under which family structure might contribute to crime.

In this respect attention was paid to the kinds of family circumstances which might contribute to persistent offending behaviour building on what was known about the way in which persistent offenders start crime early and that their offending accounts for a disproportionate amount of the total volume of crime. Utting (1993) lists those family factors as being poor parental supervision, harsh or erratic discipline, parental discord, a parent with a criminal record, low income, family size, being a low achiever at school and behaving aggressively at school. Thus Utting concludes that there is no evidence that family structure *per se* contributes to persistent offending behaviour but that perhaps more attention should be paid to families intact and the style of fathering that children are subjected to rather than freed from, echoing Currie's (1985) earlier assessment of the evidence on this issue.

This latter point connects with the second theme that this conference addressed, that is, locating an understanding of young men's criminal behaviour within the context of young men's behaviour in general rather than just within a particular family structure. This theme raised questions about men and their relationship with and expression of their masculinity. From this point of view (as was discussed in Chapter 5) the key criminological question lies in understanding, not the presence or absence of fathers, but the presence and/or absence of different ways of being a man, and how young men explore that for themselves in what might be criminal behaviour but might also be quite pleasurable risk taking behaviour (Jefferson, 1993). As Chapter 5 argued, relatively little criminological work has endeavoured to explore criminal behaviour and its underlying motivation is this kind of gendered way.

From each of these themes it is quite clear that they resonate differently with the problematic set up by the work of Dennis and Erdos and Murray; from each, different policy agendas might flow. For example, targeting persistent offenders might be addressed by an American style 'three strikes and you're out' stance, that is, if you get caught three times for any offences a long prison sentence ensues; they might be targeting by working with the families of persistent offenders; or they might be targeted by punishing the parents of persistent offenders. Each of these policy responses, from the more conservative to the more liberal, is quite different from 'demonizing' young single mothers (Tuck, 1993). In the same way targeting young men's expressions of themselves as men might be addressed through education or through 'boot camps', both of which suggest different images of what might inform an expression of 'responsibility' or responsible fatherhood. Whether a conservative or a liberal stance is adopted on this question, the outcome does not necessarily imply a return to traditional family values.

To summarize: the recent debate on the way in which the family and family structure may or may not impact upon crime highlights many of the tensions frequently experienced between what the findings of empirical work might indicate and what both popular and political opinion is prepared to tolerate. It also indicates the variety of ways in which talk about crime, and talk about what can be done about crime, can be constructed. Much of this debate has, of course, emerged from a concern about changes to family and social structure which have, by definition, been seen to be negative in their consequences.

There is an alternative viewpoint on this. As suggested earlier, many feminists might say that the number of petitions for divorce being made by women (and evidenced by Dennis and Erdos, 1992) potentially reflect a range of positive outcomes to the process of challenging traditional family structures especially for women. This is nowhere more the case than for those women and children leaving traditional family structures in which violence or rape have been a routine feature. From a point of view the modern nuclear family and its inherently patriarchal structure have never served the interests of women as human beings.

In other words, underpinning some aspects of the debate we have addressed here lies an acceptance that it is within the nuclear family that the key to individual and family harmony lies. This myth is a very powerful one in popular and political consciousness. That this does not always resonate with people's everyday experiences does not render the myth any the less powerful. It is important, however, to recognize that while the provision of stability might be one factor on which all commentators might agree can provide the optimum circumstances in which a child may avoid getting into trouble, such stability is not necessarily guaranteed by only one kind of family structure. As Smith states:

> The idea of an underclass is tied to family units of some kind: that is private associations of people who share resources and tasks (even if they don't share them fairly). It is not however tied to any particular paradigm of family structure. Family structures are, in fact, changing. The future of the underclass depends, among other things, on whether they change in a way that avoids the expansion of the group of isolated, workless, lone parents. Perhaps the family is capable of developing in more interesting and progressive ways than any that have been thought of yet.
>
> (Smith, 1992: 94)

Conclusion: questions for criminology?

The preceding discussion has endeavoured to illustrate the ways in which conceptions of social justice, that is what a particular society believes to be the fair and just distribution of the rewards and punishments in that society, can be and are connected with the processes of criminalization and the workings of the criminal justice system. Such conceptions reveal much concerning who is most likely to receive most attention from the criminal justice process, from policing the benefits system to receipt of prison sentences. These issues have been substantiated by exploring the extent to which key foundational aspects of social justice (namely how to deal with poverty and conceptions concerning the importance of the family), are embedded in historical continuities identifying those groups in society who are considered to be problematic. In addressing those foundational aspects of social justice and the ways in which they are translated into social policies which differentially target different segments of the problematic population at different points in time, several questions remain understated.

In exploring the potential relationship between gender, crime and poverty or crime, the family, and conceptions of the underclass, it is clear that one explanatory variable has been privileged in each of those explorations. Yet, at the same time, it is also clear that to do so is highly problematic. In a traditional social scientific sense, that is, in a sense which requires a search for causes so that preventive policies can be formulated, the privileging of variables in this way is, perhaps, not so difficult to appreciate. In reflecting on this discussion one may be left, quite rightly, with the difficulty of deciding whether it is gender, the changing nature of family structures, or the changing nature of social deprivation which is the root cause of criminality. Indeed, the point being that it is probably impossible, other than heuristically, to separate these variables from each other. So the examples discussed in this chapter demonstrate just how difficult it is to make such causal connections and to devise policies accordingly. It may be, for example, that the policies which have been put in place are in themselves part of the 'causal' mechanism contributing to the criminalization process.

This chapter, then, demonstrates the importance, in criminological terms, of setting any criminological agenda in a broad social and political context. At a simple level this may mean devising research agendas which resist the temptation to privilege one variable over another. At a more fundamental level it requires a rethinking of the domain assumptions of the discipline, of what it can and cannot achieve. Certainly a criminology that fails to appreciate the complex interplay between the processes of criminal justice and social justice is one likely to be impoverished in its understanding of who is most likely to receive attention from the criminal justice system, and the role that the state plays in contributing to who is made visible and who is made invisible in that process. This is not a simple call to revert to the radical criminology of the 1970s, but reflects a clear concern not to lose sight of the complex ways in which national agendas (and international agendas) are reflexively constructed. This concern reappears in Chapter 7, in which questions of victimization, as opposed to criminalization, will be more squarely addressed.

Further reading

Some of the criminological work which endeavours to formulate these links between social justice, criminal justice and criminology is to be found in the writings of Pat Carlen. Especially valuable in this respect is Carlen (1988) *Women, Crime and Poverty* and Carlen (1996) *Jigsaw: A Political*

Criminology of Youth Homelessness. Others may find that reading Murray (1990) and Dennis and Erdos (1992) is usefully thought provoking, offering a much more conservative orientation to the general question of what a just society might look like.

chapter seven

Criminal victimization, politics and welfare

What is victimology?
'Positivist' victimology
Radical victimology
Critical victimology
A challenging victimology?
Exploring repeat victimization
Conclusion: criminal victimization and social responsibility
Further reading

Studying victims has become one of the growth industries of criminology. Since 1980 there has been an extraordinarily rapid increase in national and local victim surveys and in studies of the impact of crime, of victim needs and services.

(Zedner, 1994: 1207)

As earlier chapters have illustrated, much criminological concern during the 1980s was explored through an emphasis on understanding the nature and extent of criminal victimization. This focus on the victim has different strands to it rooted to a certain extent in the different political uses to which both the term 'victim' and the image of the victim have been put. We shall endeavour to explore some of those different uses in a particular way in this chapter.

Chapter 6 considered the way in which it is possible to map interconnections between notions of social justice and the process of criminalization. This chapter will be concerned to examine those same interconnections but with a differing focus; that of understanding the process of victimization. In order to achieve this aim, this chapter will offer an overview of the different strands of victimological thought which have influenced criminology from

1979 to date (namely positivist and radical victimology) and will consider the potential for a critical victimology to constitute a better informed policy agenda on criminal victimization for the 1990s. It is via these latter concerns that the relevance of the question of the relationship between the citizen and state, considered in Chapter 6, will re-emerge. But first, what is victimology?

What is victimology?

The origins of victimology have been variously ascribed to Mendelsohn (1974) and von Hentig (1948). Arguably the work of these two writers has had the most theoretical impact on the development of victimological concerns. In some respects it was the work of von Hentig (1948) *The Criminal and his Victim* which really focused attention on the relationship between the victim and the offender in contributing to an understanding of the perpetration of a crime. Indeed, it was the early conceptual work of both Mendelsohn and von Hentig which endeavoured to establish victim typologies (a means of identifying types of victims, mirroring in some way earlier criminological concerns with types of offenders) which set the victimological agenda in two different ways. Von Hentig's work generated a concern with victim proneness, but located that concern primarily within the legal domain. Mendelsohn's work generated a concern with victim culpability arguably setting in train the much more emotive and contentious exploration of victim precipitation but located that concern within a framework which was concerned with all kinds of victimization. The legacy of each of these authors is to be found in what has been termed 'positivist' victimology on the one hand, and 'radical' victimology on the other. We shall discuss each of these in turn.

'Positivist' victimology

Miers identifies positivist victimology in the following way:

> The identification of factors which contribute to a non-random pattern of victimization, a focus on interpersonal crimes of violence, and a concern to identify victims who may have contributed to their own victimization.
>
> (Miers, 1989: 3)

The grouping of these concerns under the heading 'positivist' parallels Karmen's (1990) identification of 'conservative' victimology and Walklate's (1989) concern with a 'conventional' victimology. All of these labels capture different but important aspects of the kind of work being discussed here. This work focuses on that which is conventionally understood as criminal to the neglect of the private world of the home and the private world of the business corporation, and certainly marries well with conservative politics, an issue which will be developed shortly.

However, what underpins the surface manifestation of the characteristics variously identified by the authors above is a concern with regularities. Regularities, or patterns of behaviour, which can be identified, objectively through a commitment to a traditional conception of being 'scientific'. As has been suggested elsewhere in this text, what counts as being 'scientific' has become an increasingly contested terrain, especially in the challenge to traditional conceptions of science posed by feminist work (see, for example, Harding, 1991) and others (see, for example, MacIntyre, 1988). Despite this challenge, which largely accounts for the marginalization, and indeed alienation, of feminist work from victimology (for a fuller discussion of this see Mawby and Walklate, 1994; Walklate, 1996), this concern with regularities has been immensely influential on the focus with victims found in the political domain. This has been manifested in a number of different ways.

Initially, it was the refinement and the development of the criminal victimization survey, informed by the concept of lifestyle as articulated in the work of Hindelang *et al.* (1978) which exerted the most influence on victimology (see Mawby and Walklate, 1994: ch. 2) and its utility in the political domain. As earlier chapters have demonstrated, the criminal victimization survey as a research instrument has been harnessed by academic work on both the right and the left of the criminological political spectrum. In the context of the discussion here, the findings of such surveys have been used by political conservatives both to downplay the risk of crime (see Hough and Mayhew, 1983) and to emphasize the risk of crime (see The United States President's Task Force on Victims of Crime, 1982).

So, arguably, the patterns and regularities revealed by positivistic victimology have been used both expediently and to some effect in the political arena. The connections between this kind of victimology and a more general political conservatism, however, run somewhat deeper than the mere political manipulation and utilization of survey findings. They are connections which emanate from the image of the victim and the presumptions about the nature of society which positivistic victimology makes.

The three characteristics of positive victimology offered by Miers (1989) with which this section began are underpinned by a presumption that the term victim itself is non-problematic. In various forms of victimological work conducted within this vein, the victim is taken to be given either by the criminal law or by the self-evident nature of the victim's suffering. Such a starting point enables the generation of data concerned with patterns and regularities since it presumes that what there is to be measured can in fact be measured and in itself is a static entity.

As has been argued elsewhere (Walklate, 1989), this initial presumption conceals an inherently static and functionalist view of society in which the themes of consensus, equilibrium and incremental change are predominant. There is little sense in this image of society or the individual in which the law or the state contributes to the social construction of the victim, the processes of criminal victimization, or processes of social change which may be unforeseen and/or dramatic as opposed to managed and incremental. So positivist victimology, and the survey work emanating from it, may provide snapshots of regularities of criminal victimization but cannot provide an understanding of the social and historical reproduction of those regularities through time and space. Such a concern demands minimally a different understanding of the term victim, and maximally a different theoretical starting point.

However, this non-problematic treatment of the notion of the victim offers one way of thinking through those other connections with political conservatism. Karmen expresses some of those connections:

> Conservatives within victimology and the victims' rights movement see the criminal justice system as the guarantor of retributive justice – satisfying victims with the knowledge that offenders are being punished for their crimes.
>
> (Karmen, 1990: 11)

It is to this end that the 'powerful motif' of the victim, commented on by Bottoms (1983), was put to most effective use in the UK through the 1980s and 1990s. On occasion such use has been led by victims' organizations, as was the case with the 'Victims of Violence' group in the early 1980s (Jonkers, 1986), on other occasions especially in the 1990s it has been government led (see, for example, the 'Prison works' speech given to the Conservative Party Conference by the then Home Secretary Michael Howard in September 1993).

As Phipps (1988) has argued, the politicization of the victim in this way has led to a separation of the notion of criminal victimization from its *social* (my emphasis) origins seeing it as something which interferes with the 'normality' of an ordered society. He goes on to say that

> Further, the interventionist State must share the blame, for it has weakened authority of all kinds as well as tying the hands of the police and the courts by placing the rights of offenders above the rights of potential and actual victims to be free from harm and fear.
>
> (Phipps, 1988: 180)

The argument developed by Phipps (1988) suggests that what Conservatism does is to transform the harm caused to individuals as a result of criminal victimization into a harming of the social order, of the rule of law, and of 'community'. In policy terms this does indeed translate into a general commitment to repressive justice which can take a number of different forms.

Moreover, as Young (1996) argues, the use of the term 'victim' in the political domain serves more purposes that just a need to generate support for a particular policy initiative or direction. Those other purposes serve to signify the ideological mechanisms whereby the term victim acts as both a strategy for including 'all of us' yet simultaneously excluding the criminal. Such purposes, however, are not solely the prerogative of conservative politicians. Signifying the victim in this way is equally problematic for that victimology which sees itself as being of a more radical persuasion.

Radical victimology

Arguably radical victimology has its origins in the work of Mendelsohn (1974) who, despite the more conservative implications of other aspects of his ideas, argued for a victimology concerned with all aspects of victimization, not just those which could be defined as criminal. This concern can be traced through the work of both radical criminology (Quinney, 1972) as well as radical victimology (Elias, 1986, 1993).

The common threads which bind these different strands of work together can be identified as a concern with the role of the state alongside the law in producing victimization. These threads connect this version of victimology to a concern with the question of human rights. As Elias states:

> A victimology which encompasses human rights would not divert attention from crime victims and their rights, but would rather explore their inextricable relationship to more universal human rights concerns.
>
> (Elias, 1985: 17)

Such concerns readily connect the radical victimologist with the victims' movement through organizations such as Amnesty International, for example. However, in the more localized political domain of party politics in the UK during the 1980s, it was arguably the ideas of radical victimology which underpinned some of the concerns of the radical left realists discussed in Chapter 4.

As Chapter 4 discussed and as has been commented on elsewhere (Smart, 1990; Mawby and Walklate, 1994), radical left realism in particular and radical victimology in general fail to escape the chains of a positivistic conception of science. Thus while the underpinning focus of radical victimology on questions of human rights might be considered laudable their translation into standards which can be measured objectively, as articulated in the work of Elias for example, remains problematic. Moreover, the recognition of the power of the state and the law to oppress, which offers a less than consensual image of the relationship between the individual and society, has had a more rhetorical impact on politics than a 'real' one perhaps with the exception of radical left realism in the UK.

As Chapter 4 demonstrated, radical left realism argues for what has been called an 'engaged' criminology. In England this has been reflected in an association between 'left realist' criminologists and some Labour controlled local authorities, primarily in London, in an effort to reclaim the debate on law and order for the Labour Party. In very general terms these efforts present a different conceptualization of victimization. As Phipps points out,

> criminal victimization is but one aspect of *social* victimization arising from poverty and disadvantage – in which people are harmed by *normal* social and economic relations, a process which in turn results in their harming each other.
>
> (Phipps, 1988: 181)

Part of the consequence of endeavouring to reclaim the law and order debate in this way, has led radical left realism to elide the concern with crime with a concern with criminal victimization. As Young (1996) argues, this elision equates victimization with citizenship. This issue is worth developing a little more fully.

As Chapter 4 illustrated, one of the criticisms made of left realism lies in its use of the notion of crime as a unified and a unifying category. One of the implications of this use is the idea that crime is a 'leveller'. Young expresses this in this way;

> It [crime] provides a sense of community . . . But our belonging comes not from the fact that we are all criminals but from the shared fact of victimization.
>
> (Young, 1996: 55)

This sense of common victimization providing a basis to belonging may be differently distributed by space, age, race or gender, but it is nevertheless the means through which 'all of us' as potential victims can be harnessed to participate in the democratic process. Thus our potential victimization acts as a mechanism whereby our activities as citizens can also be harnessed.

It is not only left realism which has connoted the term victim in this way. The 1980s, characterized as it has been by Karmen (1990) as being signified in policy terms as a move from crime prevention to victimization prevention, saw those of both a left wing and a right wing political persuasion collude in the construction of a notion of social responsibility in relation to crime control in terms of victimization reduction. Indeed, the intervention of left realism, albeit brief, into the debate on citizenship argued for a social individualism which considered not only the rights of the citizen but their obligations too. Such a conception of citizenship is not that far removed from that identified in Chapter 6, the notion of 'active citizenship'.

Thus it can be seen that while radical victimology tries to construct and work with a much more general notion of victimization and with a relatively subtle and nuanced understanding of the sources of such victimization, its failure to break free of positivism at a fundamental level results in a political agenda not that dissimilar in its presumptions from that of a more conservative political persuasion. Efforts have been made to break free of this conundrum through the construction of what has been called 'critical victimology'. It is to a consideration of that work which we shall now turn.

Critical victimology

The term 'critical' has been used by a number of different writers to delineate an alternative way of thinking about the nature of victimization. Miers (1990), for example, uses it to draw attention to the process of acquiring both the label and status of victim. Fattah (1992) uses it to call for a better integration of criminological and victimological knowledge. The way in which this term has been used by Walklate (1990) and Mawby and Walklate (1994), however, denotes a substantially different theoretical and empirical starting place than either positive or radical victimology and subsequently leads to a different conceptualization of the relationship between the citizen and the state. We shall consider each of these issues in turn.

Critical victimology as articulated in the work of Walklate (1990) and Mawby and Walklate (1994) takes as its starting point the need to understand what constitutes the 'real'. Influenced by the work of Bhaskar (1978) and Giddens (1984), this form of victimology centres on the need for an empirically informed policy agenda, but one which is as concerned with that which 'goes on behind our backs' as it is with that which we can see. Drawing explicitly on the theoretical work of Giddens, this concern implies the need to take account of a number of processes which contribute to the construction of everyday life:

> people's conscious activity, their 'unconscious' activity (that is, routine activities people engage in which serve to sustain and sometimes change, the conditions in which they act), the generative mechanisms (unobservable and unobserved) which underpin daily life, and finally, both the intended and the unintended consequences of action which feed back into people's knowledge.
>
> (Mawby and Walklate, 1994: 19)

A theoretical starting point such as this one carries with it a number of implications for not only what kind of empirical investigation is most likely to reveal the processes outlined above (comparative and longitudinal) but also what might constitute the central concerns of such an area of analysis.

In the context of criminal victimization, Mawby and Walklate (1994) have argued that the kind of theoretical starting point outlined above not only generates a challenge to the domain assumptions of victimology as a discipline, but also generates a concern with three key policy oriented concepts – rights, citizenship and the state. It has been seen that these concepts are also intimately connected with other versions of victimology so we shall consider the nature of their interrelationship in this context too. What matters, of course, is to understand how they might be differently interpreted and harnessed in the political process. In other words, what gives this version of victimology its critical policy edge?

Articulating an understanding of the relationship between citizen and state can be predicated on a range of different assumptions. In the context of critical victimology those assumptions have been informed by some of the ways in which different strands of feminist thought raise questions about what is implied in the concept of the citizen and the state and the relationship between the two. As the analysis by Barbelet (1988) demonstrates, the relationship between citizen and state is neither easy nor straightforward but in the final analysis, however, the struggle between the citizen and the state is conceptualized, the state ultimately grants or denies its citizens their rights. So it is to an understanding of the concept of the state that we shall turn first of all.

Critical victimology presumes that the state is not necessarily neutral nor benign in its activities. Such a view stems from the work of Offe (1984). Appreciating the ways in which the state operates sometimes in the interests of its citizens, but always in the interests of self-maintenance, is central to understanding the underlying (generative) mechanisms that contribute towards the kinds of victimizations which we 'see' as compared to those which we do not 'see'. The way in which the term 'victim' has been used symbolically in the political arena has already been commented on in this chapter and elsewhere. Perhaps what has not been sufficiently outlined is the way in which the notion of the victim as delineating 'all of us' also serves ideological purposes especially at times when the state is economically less well secure.

Offe and Ronge (1975) argue that as the contradictions within welfare state capitalism have become increasingly acute, the stability of the state could be maintained only by 'creating the conditions under which legal and economic subjects' could function as commodities. Arguably the processes which have occurred within the UK from the mid-1970s have constituted an effort to 'commodify' citizenship. This has been embodied in a number of different ways, but what is clear is that by the 1990s the citizen as consumer had become well embedded in social and criminal justice policy. This is illustrated by the (earlier) development and growth of Neighbourhood Watch schemes to the (later) introduction of 'Quality of Service' units by some police forces. Indeed, one way of understanding the apparent increase of police activity with respect to 'domestic' violence from 1990 onwards is to recast women as consumers of a police service whose evaluations of that service might feed into performance indicators.

Embodying the citizen as a consumer of services not only serves to 'justify' the levels of expenditure available for those services, but also serves to maintain at an ideological level a notion of both the citizen and the state as being neutral entities. As MacKinnon has cogently argued, the state under discussion here is a patriarchal state:

> The liberal state coercively and authoritatively constitutes the social order in the interests of men as a gender – through its legitimating norms, forms, relation to society, and substantive policies.
>
> (MacKinnon, 1989: 162)

Not only is the state gendered, but also it is embedded in notions of class and race which permeate its activities. This is no more nor less the case than in the area of the law (see Naffine, 1990). This does not mean that the state cannot be challenged. What it does imply, however, is that any challenge posed to the state and its activities of self-maintenance may not always have the 'progressive' outcome intended. Matthews (1994) for example, comments on the way in which the adoption of feminist informed rape crisis programmes has in some circumstances resulted in their co-option by the state. Smart (1989) raises a similar dilemma for feminists who look to changing the law as a way of enhancing women's rights before the law. Such an outcome is not always or necessarily guaranteed.

For this version of critical victimology, then, the state is not an objective, neutral arbiter of the 'facts' but a self-interested and self-motivated mechanism in which its interests at different historical moments may be more or less paramount dependent upon economic circumstances (echoing some of the themes addressed in Chapter 2). This does not mean that the state always remains impervious to questions of gender, race or class, but it does mean that in order to understand the ways in which those questions may or may not be articulated in policy terms are connected with the underlying activities of the state itself. These, then, set the scene in which some aspects of citizenship becomes visible and other remain invisible.

One which has remained invisible, and which was commented on earlier, is the way in which, as Young (1996) observes, victimization has become elided with citizenship:

> If everyone is a victim, then everyone has a part to play in the struggle against crime. More strongly, everyone has a *duty*: it is part of the offices of the citizen to minimize the risk of becoming a victim.
>
> (Young, 1996: 56, emphasis as original)

This elision between victimization captures the commonality between left wing and right wing criminology/victimology on this issue, despite the surface manifestation of political differences. These have been presented as social rights and social obligations like the right to work articulated by the left realists as opposed to active citizenship and social responsibility emanating from the right to property of those on the right. Such political differences fail to address the fundamental elision observed above and consequently fail to consider conceptions of citizenship which are collective in origin as opposed to possessed by individuals (Mouffe, 1988).

A continued commitment to a discourse on the question of citizenship rooted in notions of individualism simultaneously serves to blame, if not hide, those collectivities whose economic and material conditions have been worsening (relatively) since 1979. A critically informed victimology is one which is concerned to understand the mechanisms whereby such collectivities are hidden and what might constitute the real policy opportunities, economic circumstances notwithstanding, to equip those collectivities with 'rights'.

This is not the place to offer a picture of what such a policy agenda might concern itself with (for a detailed discussion of this see Mawby and Walklate, 1994: ch. 9). Needless to say such a policy agenda is one which does not privilege the notion of victims' rights but considers those policy possibilities which might ensure a more equitable experience of the criminal justice process for all groups of people who might come into contact with it. A key concern of critical victimology, then, is to challenge the use of the term 'victim' and the circumstances under which such a term may be applicable. In so doing it constitutes a fundamental challenge to the domain assumptions of victimology as a discipline. An appreciation of that challenge will facilitate a deeper understanding of both the theoretical and policy agenda of a critical victimology.

A challenging victimology?

As the concerns of this chapter have demonstrated, victimology shares an implicitly parallel, though chronologically later, history with criminology. Those parallels are present in the delineation of different emphases within the discipline – positivist, radical and critical. Labels which are readily identifiable within the criminological domain. However, the parallels between these two areas of concern are somewhat deeper than this. They share not only a 'catholic' character (Rock, 1986) but also a fundamental commitment to the three concerns of differentiation, pathology, and determinism. (On the influence of these on criminology see Taylor et al., 1973; Roshier, 1989.) Taken together, alongside a commitment to a traditional view of the 'scientific', these concerns have formed the bedrock of criminology as a discipline. What has been less well articulated is the way in which these concerns, especially that of differentiation, have also constituted the bedrock of victimology.

As was stated earlier, the work of Mendelsohn (1974) and von Hentig (1948) is frequently taken as the starting point for victimological concerns. While neither of these writers intended to suggest that there was such a being as the 'born victim', they were nevertheless searching for ways of *differentiating* the potential victim from the non-victim which could be applied in all victimizing situations. This concern with differentiation is clearly consonant with the work of the early criminologists.

Later versions of this kind of work are much more sophisticated than those of von Hentig and Mendelsohn, but they nevertheless share in the early criminological worldview that if criminals could be identified in some way then so could victims. Not only could they be identified, but more often than not they were identifiable by some personal characteristic which marked the victim as being different from the norm. What constituted that norm was differently interpreted for different writers, but what they shared in common was an underlying presumption that that normality was characterized by the white, heterosexual male (see Walklate, 1995: ch. 2).

In this way victimology, unsurprisingly, shared in those fundamental tenets of early criminology – determinism, differentiation and pathology. These concerns are reflected in the work of the early victimologists whose typologies focused on either the personal characteristics of the victim (whether they were female, old, mentally defective, etc., for von Hentig) or the contribution that their behaviour made to the commission of a crime (from being totally innocent to the criminal who became the victim, for Mendelsohn). They are also reflected in the subsequent development of the discipline and its focus on the concepts of victim precipitation and lifestyle.

These two concepts, victim precipitation and lifestyle, constitute the core of much victimological thinking, as has been alluded to in this chapter. As concepts they have generated a significant amount of empirical work and consequently have contributed to the development of the victimological agenda. As concepts they also both implicitly and explicitly focus our attention on the behaviour of individual victims. Indeed Fattah (1991), in reviewing the available data and explanations for differential patterns of victimization, attempts to integrate a range of victimological work generated in this way into a general schema. In doing so he groups forty propositions about criminal victimization under ten key headings: available opportunities, risk factors, the presence of motivated offenders, exposure, associations, dangerous times/dangerous places, dangerous behaviours, high risk activities, defensive/avoidance behaviours and structural cultural proneness. This listing, while evidently more sophisticated than the simplistic assertion of a notion of lifestyle or victim precipitation, still reflects the central influence that these concepts have had on victimology. But more importantly, they all, with one exception, direct attention to trying to differentiate the (potential) victim's behaviour.

This concern to differentiate victims from others, whether in terms of their personal or their behavioural characteristics, has constituted a key assumption of much victimological work. A critical victimology, as outlined above, clearly challenges the presumption that victims can be differentiated in this way. Critical victimology articulates the view that it is within the routine practices of everyday life that the processes of 'victimization' are produced and reproduced. How this is expressed might be best explored by examining the implication of a popular policy initiative of the 1990s – repeat victimization.

Exploring repeat victimization

> Research has shown that repeatedly victimised people and places account for a significant proportion of all crime. One study found that of the 1992 British Crime Survey respondents, half of those who were victimized were repeat victims and suffered 81 per cent of all reported crimes. Of these 4 per cent were chronically victimized. That is, they suffered four or more crimes in a year, and accounted for 44 per cent of all the reported crime. Effectively preventing crime against these people and places should ultimately have an overall impact on crime levels.
>
> (Wise After the Event: Tackling Repeat Victimization, National Board for Crime Prevention, May, 1994: 2)

Targeting the phenomenon of 'repeat victimization' has become an increasingly popular feature in the struggle to combat a rising crime rate. Such a policy focus is, arguably, a logical outcome of what Karmen (1990) has identified as a move away from crime prevention towards an emphasis on victimization prevention, a process which has characterized much crime prevention activity in England and Wales, particularly since 1979. For the most part this change in emphasis has proceeded with relatively little criticism though, in a general policy context, it perhaps makes 'good sense' in crime prevention terms to target the chronically victimized given an economic framework of ever tightening resources. The questions arise, of course, as to what underpins such a policy directive and could there be an alternative. It is at this juncture that the relationship between theory and practice re-emerges. An appreciation of the use of the term 'multiple' or 'repeat' victim will facilitate an understanding of this.

Farrell (1992) has endeavoured to document the genealogy of the term 'multiple victim'. As a concept it appears to have been first used by Johnson et al. (1973) in *The Recidivist Victim: A Decriptive Study*. However, as Farrell (1992) goes on to point out, Hindelang et al. (1978) also devoted some time to the phenomenon of multiple victimization in support of their life-style exposure model, as did Sparks et al. (1977). This latter piece of work afforded the opportunity for one of the researchers, Genn, to return to one of the London boroughs in which this first criminal victimization survey work was conducted in order to engage in some supplementary participant observation work. Published in 1988 this study offers some insights into the tensions between conventional victim survey work informed by the lifestyle model and how people actually routinely experience criminal victimization. It is worth quoting Genn (1988) at length on this:

> Becoming interested in what appeared to be examples of 'victim-prone-ness' in one geographical area, I visited one particular block on a council estate over a number of months, tape-recorded interviews with several families, their neighbours and friends, and eventually moved in for a short period with the woman who had suffered the greatest number of victimizations in our survey. The views which I formed after this period of intensive observation have a substantial bearing not simply on the experiences of multiple victims but on the limitations of victim surveys as they are currently designed . . . What also became apparent was the fact that events reported to us in the survey were not regarded as particularly remarkable. *They were just a part of life.*
>
> (Genn, 1988: 92–3, added emphasis)

As Farrell's (1992) review of the literature on multiple victimization documents, and Genn (1988) implies, much of the focus of the work in this area has been 'event' oriented and individual centred. Indeed, despite Farrell's (1992) persistent recognition of the 'unfortunate' victim blaming connotations underpinning multiple victimization work, that work has proceeded to work within these foci, Genn's (1988) caveats notwithstanding.

This is largely a consequence of the powerful influence of the lifestyle exposure model and its implicit concern with differentiation, which underpins the victim survey work and from which the data illustrating the nature and extent of multiple victimization is drawn. However, as Genn's (1988) analysis implies, there is at least one other way of thinking about multiple victimizations: 'They were just a part of life'. What might a view such as this imply theoretically?

Genn's (1988) analysis of living with a multiple victimized woman in 'Bleak House' could have been drawn from a whole range of studies which have been concerned to document the nature of many women's routine lives. Largely located within feminist analyses that literature refuses to adopt an individualized event oriented approach to women's experiences (including their experiences of criminal victimization) preferring instead to locate an understanding of such experiences within the reality of women's routine lives in relation to men that they know. Put more simply, this latter approach privileges processes over events. In some respects then, feminist work, especially on 'domestic' violence for example, articulates an understanding, par excellence, of the processes surrounding multiple victimization.

There has been some recognition of the importance of these processes by those heavily involved in the multiple victimization debate. However, this recognition is largely marred by the fact that the feminist model noted above has been incorporated into a 'routine activities' perspective (as discussed in Chapter 2). So the work of Farrell and others displays, at a minimum, a degree of inconsistency between the desire to move away from the connotation of victim-precipitation – and victim blaming which the targeting of 'multiple victims' implies – yet they retain a commitment to a theoretical framework which inhibits their ability to do so. In particular, their account of the repetition of victimization turns on being able to differentiate repeat victims, either by prior risk or subsequent risk history, that is, as being 'suitable targets' for repetitive criminal behaviour.

So the argument developed by Hope and Walklate (1995) concerned to critique this work was that the legacy of differentiation inherited from positive criminology, read across into victimology, is now being applied to repeat victimization. This legacy privileges outcome – the victimization event – over process – the victimizing relationship – as the focus of study. This approach seeks to differentiate victim risk on a priori grounds, that is, as a property of individuals or targets, with these properties resulting in their subsequent exposure to risk.

Hope and Walklate (1995) argue that such an approach represents only a partial conceptualization of the process since it focuses mainly on the 'first' victimization. In other words, in this formulation, differentiation of the victim is achieved in the moments following the victimizing event. In contrast, Hope and Walklate (1995) suggest that various 'victimizing relationships' have structural properties which shape their duration over time and space in ways which cannot be entirely reduced merely to the subsequent reinforcement of a priori individual risk. Such an argument returns us to the theorizing of Giddens (summarized above) which also underpins the formulation of a critical victimology offered here.

One of the basic premises on which these theoretical propositions are constructed is the notion of duality; that is an emphasis on the *interrelationship* between agency and structure. Crucially, this is a dynamic relationship over time-space. This provides one way of understanding the dynamism between, for example, the structural location of women (one way of understanding women's powerlessness, a defining characteristic of being a victim), and women's negotiation of their structural location (one way of understanding the term 'survivor'). It is this kind of theoretical starting point, which neither treats individual characteristics as given nor individual events as products of such givens, which permits the development of a critical edge to the work on repeat victimization. As Hope and Walklate state:

> Yet it may be that all victimisation has a potential for repetition; the crucial point being why do many avoid it. Arguably, a focus on

victim-precipitation and differentiation has obscured defining aspects of victimisation, especially issues of power and dominance in personal and social relations, which a focus on the structuration of victimisation, and its routinization, clarifies.

(Hope and Walklate, 1995: 18, emphasis as original)

The consequence of these theoretical concerns may be that it is the *processes* underpinning 'domestic' violence, bullying, racial attacks, which are the 'normal' case of victimization, and it is the 'one-off' victimizing event which is much more difficult to explain. If this is the case, then, the targeting of repeat victims, predicated as it is on the notion that these are somehow different than other forms of victimization, is not only theoretically misplaced but in policy and resource effectiveness terms is only ever going to be at best partially successful.

Of course, as several chapters in this book have demonstrated, it is understanding how the mechanisms of crime and victimization work, and what might constitute the appropriate moments of intervention which comprise the key empirical tasks of not only victimology but also criminology. In this much Fattah's (1992) call to break down the barriers between the two disciplines may be correct if his work simultaneously offers a limited theoretical framework within which to achieve this. Moreover, what this chapter has demonstrated so far is the way in which the more recent concern with criminal victimization found in both the world of criminal justice policy and academia has been predicated on the powerful influence of a particular image and understanding of the victim. As the conclusion will suggest, the success of this image is intimately connected with the changing conception of welfare to be found within the political domain.

Conclusion: criminal victimization and social responsibility

As Chapter 6 argued, the distribution of the rewards and punishments in any society is predicated upon some notion of what is considered to be 'socially just'. The way in which that has been constructed in the UK since the late 1940s has been for the most part translated into a conception of the 'welfare state'. Chapter 6 also articulated some views on the ways in which conceptions of the welfare state have changed in emphasis since the late 1940s and how those changes in conceptions of welfare could be connected to the processes of criminalization.

This chapter has been concerned to address a different though connected thread in those processes. Here we have been concerned to document explicitly the different strands of thought found within the disciplinary concerns of victimology, and the ways in which those strands of thought connect in different ways with the world of politics. What remains is to make explicit the ways in which these concerns are also connected to images of a socially just society.

Young (1996) has offered the view that the image of the victim used both academically and politically in the 1980s and after clearly served exclusionary and inclusionary purposes. It would certainly appear to be the case that criminal justice rhetoric on citizenship has been rooted in a notion of potential victimization. Such potential victimization carries with it implications for both individuals and individual communities.

Walklate (1992) has argued that crime prevention policy during the 1980s was embedded in a framework of blame: offender blaming, victim blaming and community blaming, none of which was (or is) necessarily mutually exclusive categories in terms of policy but they are labels which do capture both the content and direction of crime prevention policy during that period. Underpinning them are the same conceptions of the relationship between the individual and the state which underpinned other aspects of social policy at that time and since, namely a reduction in the role of the state and an enhancement of the role of the individual in delivering the overall welfare of both.

The changing balance between the state and the individual has been described in different ways, from the removal of the 'nanny state' and the 'dependency culture' to the rise of possessive individualism. However this process is described and whatever moral connotations such descriptions invoke, its impact in terms of criminal victimization has not only been symbolic (the invocation of victimization as 'belonging') but also been material. This is identifiable in the practices of insurance companies in relation to claims as a result of household burglary, in the counting of income from a Criminal Injuries Compensation claim as income for social security purposes, to the withdrawal of services from those communities specifically defined as problematic (Campbell, 1993).

In other words, there is a real sense in which the drive to enhance social responsibility in this individualized form of 'active citizenship' and/or consumerism takes its toll on those sections of society least able to afford it. This 'fact' is recognized by both conservative and liberal criminologists in the UK and the United States. Where they differ, of course, is in their explanation of its underlying cause and what is likely to improve it. But few would disagree that the changing relationship between citizen and state has done little to alleviate the lot of the 'dangerous classes'.

There is a sense, then, in which this concern with criminal victimization, the different strands of which have been documented in this chapter, return us to consider the ways in which the same sections of society not only are targeted in terms of criminalization but also are made to pay disproportionately in terms of victimization. Arguably, much more theoretical and empirical work needs to be done focusing on the ways in which these processes are stitched together. But for now it is perhaps sufficient to observe that if there is any mileage left in criminology's commitment to the modernist project, that mileage may lie in embracing more fully the implications of developing a more careful understanding of the interconnections between criminal justice and social justice.

Further reading

Victimology as an area of study has certainly grown over the last decade. Various attempts have been made to document these developments, for example, Walklate (1989) *Victimology: The Victim and the Criminal Justice Process* and Mawby and Walklate (1994) *Critical Victimology: The Victim in International Perspective.* For a different orientation on understanding victimization, Elias (1993) *Victims Still: The Political Manipulation of Crime Victims* provides a provocative account of the interconnections between levels of victimization and the associated political choices. The book of readings edited by Maguire and Pointing (1988) *Victims of Crime: A New Deal?* still provides a sound feel for the different concerns of those who populate the victims' movement.

chapter eight

Conclusion: new directions for criminology?

Positivism, modernism and gender
Criminology and risk
Criminology and trust
Criminology, the citizen and the state
Conclusion

This book has endeavoured to explore different ways that talk about crime has been constructed. It has in that process paid some attention to the way in which those different ways of talking about crime have rendered some conceptual issues more visible than others. It has also paid some attention to the way in which the political domain informs criminological theorizing and sometimes directs that theorizing. The outcome of which has frequently been reflected in the policy arena. In this conclusion we shall revisit some of these issues in a slightly different form as a way of reasserting some of the themes that have been foregrounded in the previous chapters and as a way of introducing some newer ways of thinking about the criminological agenda. In order to do this we shall revisit in the first instance three recurring and interconnected issues addressed in this text: they are positivism, modernism and gender.

Positivism, modernism and gender

The influence of positivism on the criminological agenda has been profound. The desire to produce and work with the objectively measurable facts of crime, as has been shown, is intimately connected with the emergence of criminology as a 'modern' social science. It is also intimately connected with the subject matter of the discipline itself and the diversity of interests which people the discipline.

Lawbreaking behaviour, to a greater or lesser degree, can be measured. Some lawbreaking behaviours are more hidden than others. Some behaviours can be newly defined as lawbreaking. Moreover, there may well be a complex definitional process which contributes to the behaviour which is seen and not seen. However, at the end of the day, there is something measurable here, which in some respects is more easily measurable than 'social relationships' or the 'structure of society'. Criminal behaviour is real and it is real in its consequences. That is not to say that the social relationships and/or social structures are not real, but merely to emphasize the powerful impact that the observable nature of criminal behaviour has had on the nature of the discipline itself.

In some respects the material reality of crime, however accurately it is measured, has served to fuel the hold that positivism has had on the criminological agenda. Counting crime, and the work of the criminal justice agencies, is in some respects the bedrock of criminological investigation. The presence of this bedrock has been felt in a number of different ways; from the mind imaging of neuroscience to the geographically focused criminal victimization survey of the left realist. Each in their own way endeavouring to contribute to the objective measurement of the phenomenon of crime, and each in their own way contributing to the further perpetuation of the power of positivism. However, what underpins the continued influence of positivism is perhaps more fundamental than this discussion has so far implied.

The continued, almost implicit, acceptance of the ideas of positivism within criminology, also reflects the discipline's intimate connection with the ideas of modernism. Borne out of the Enlightenment, the modern society was conceived as being that society in which decisions were made which were rooted in rational knowledge rather than superstition or belief. Positivism, the gathering of information about that which could be observed, as opposed to that which could be felt or believed, constituted the main strategy though which rational knowledge could be constructed. From this kind of knowledge, policies could be formulated which might contribute to the better management of social change. In this latter respect, the fundamental concerns of mainstream criminological work have changed little since the days of Lombroso. Of course, what is embedded in these ideas is a set of presumptions around what counts as rational knowledge and who can possess such knowledge as much as they reflect ideas around how that knowledge is to be gathered.

Implicit in the modern, positive view of social reality is a presumption that human experience and male experience are one and the same. Seidler (1994) has argued that the implicit acceptance of this view has had a profound effect on social theory, and it is easy to see that same profound effect upon criminological theory (see Chapter 5).

It is for men to be the guardians of 'reason' and 'objectivity' and so to refuse to be drawn into the unbounded and the chaotic, that, like the feminine, can so easily overwhelm. Social theory and philosophy have to stay within the limits of reason, learning to stay within the province of what can be clearly said.

(Seidler, 1994: 202)

The influence of hegemonic masculinity, embedded within the discipline of criminology, has been commented on elsewhere by Scraton (1990). The significance of recognizing the gendered base to knowledge, however, runs much deeper than a desire to think more carefully about how research agendas are constructed or sampling procedures put in place, as the critique of left realism in Chapter 4 demonstrates.

Recognition of the gendered base to knowledge demands a critical assessment and recognition of the ways in which the concepts used and deployed within criminology and victimology may not fully resonate with human experience. In other words, it requires a critical examination of the ways in which these concepts may articulate a male view of the world, not conspiratorially, but in a taken for granted way which (potentially) sets the agenda for the discipline in a particular (and limiting) way. Given this interplay between positivism, modernism and gender, it is no wonder that some have looked to developing theoretical and conceptual concerns for criminology which emanate from agendas outside of criminology rather than continue to struggle with the powerful influence of its internal agenda.

To summarize: the emergence of the modern form of criminology, and the context in which that occurred, ties the discipline to traditional conceptions of knowledge and traditional conceptions of what counts as rational knowledge. Once it is recognized that these interconnections have a gendered base, then it is possible to appreciate why it is that feminism (and the more recent work on masculinities) represents such a profound challenge for the discipline of criminology. At a minimum this challenge suggests that there is a different way of working with the relationship between what might be considered scientific and what might be considered rational. The implications of such alternatives challenge criminology in a number of different ways.

The challenge to the conventional link between science, rationality and the policy agenda, which has been a recurring theme in this book, has come not only from those exploring gender issues but also from those working with the postmodernist ideas. Both of these standpoints, when applied to understanding knowledge and the knowledge production process, challenge the traditional universalism associated with traditional conceptions of science. The critique of left realism (and right realism) from those working within postmodernism evidences this. Challenging universalism implies (at a minimum) that knowledge is relative.

The resistance towards accepting knowledge as relative is present in both criminology and victimology. This is not only a result of an underlying search for the cause of crime and the tension that this text has evidenced as still being present between those who wish to centre the individual and those who wish to centre the social as the locus in which the cause of crime can be found, but also the result of the drive to produce policies. Moreover, to produce policies that work.

This is not to suggest that the search for causes and for effective policies are as a consequence fruitless, if the relativity of knowledge is accepted. However, it does suggest that such a search and such policies might be much more specifically and locally nuanced than has hitherto been the case. Arguably though, it is necessary for both criminology and victimology to engage in a much more self-reflexive critique with respect to the conceptual apparatus within which they both operate, before this position can be reached.

Thus the challenge of both feminism and postmodernism to the traditional implicit relationship between science, modernism and gender found in both criminology and victimology constitutes more than a polemical call for an appreciation of the relative nature of knowledge and the knowledge production process. It also requires a critical consideration of what is and is not made visible and invisible in the conceptual and research agendas which are constructed within these disciplines. This is necessary not only in relation to questions of gender, but also in relation to questions of class, race, age, community, etc. Whose knowledge counts, how and why?

One way to begin to map an understanding of these processes is to render more explicit other taken for granted aspects of the way in which criminology and victimology have constructed their frameworks for understanding crime. The analysis offered here will endeavour to achieve this by exploring the pertinence of understanding risk, trust and the relationship between the citizen and the state for the future development of both criminology and victimology.

Criminology and risk

In the mid-1980s Short made the following observations on criminology and modern risk analysis:

> The technical aspects of crime management and the management of risks to human health and life have much in common. In the latter, levels of risk are determined, often without firm knowledge of results which might follow from policies based on them, or of causal processes ... Distinctions between causation and control, and between determination of risks and judgements of safety, are neither straightforward nor simple. The results of neglect of such distinctions are

similar for risk analysis and for criminology. Separation of causal theory and research from social policy in both areas condemns the latter to the treatment of symptoms.

(Short, 1984: 713)

Here Short is drawing attention to a number of significant features not only associated with the social sciences but also associated with modern life in general.

A deep rooted social expectation associated with the exponential growth of scientific knowledge appears to be a presumption that (modern) life should no longer be risky. Such cultural values pervade the issues of health, of the food we eat, of the leisure activities we engage in, through to what we expect the 'professionals' in each of these domains to be able to provide for us. The concepts of risk and risk assessment increasingly inform such public perceptions and have certainly informed the criminological agenda. For example, the phenomenon of repeat victimization, discussed in Chapter 7, has at its heart the presumption that being able to identify those most at risk from criminal victimization will not only aid in its prevention but also as a corollary constitute a more cost effective use of resources. But as Short acknowledges, and as the critical analysis of repeat victimization as discussed in this text implies, that leaves criminology dealing with the symptoms of crime rather than its causes. (Interestingly enough risk assessment has been largely absent from criminological discussions of corporate crime or fraud, an issue to which we shall return.)

Working with the concept of risk and risk assessment in this way is clearly connected to the notions of a (masculinist) science embedded within criminology and victimology discussed above. As a consequence these characteristics have resulted in the implicit acceptance of the idea of risk within criminology as a forensic concept. In other words there has been an acceptance that in the possibility of understanding risk and risk analysis lies risk management. The control of outcomes: the control of probabilities which determine the likely consequences of particular courses of action. This is, as Douglas (1992) argues, what is culturally expected from the scientific enterprise. There are a number of both general and specific difficulties in criminology's continued acceptance of the concept of risk formulated in this way.

A general problem raised by the risk analysis industry is offered by Bernstein (1996). As he says, 'The past seldom obliges by revealing to us when wildness will break out in the future' (Bernstein, 1996: 334). This quote clarifies the basis on which risk assessments are made. In other words, probability theory, rooted as it is in historical data, can only ever be just that – theory. Events can always happen otherwise, despite cultural values and beliefs to the contrary. Of course, in a sense this is precisely the purpose of risk management: to minimize the impact of events happening otherwise. It cannot, however, eliminate their possible occurrence. This is as effectively the case for crime as it is for any other social problem in which risk assessment is considered salient.

While the notion of 'wildness' might draw attention to the ultimate ineffectiveness of trying to predict and/or control outcomes, it does not necessarily facilitate an understanding of the risks we see as opposed to the risks we do not see. As Beck (1992) and Wildavsky (1988) both argue, this latter process is also culturally constructed; and culturally constructed as much to hide the extent to which the scientific enterprise has contributed to rising levels of risk as well as finding ways to control such levels of risk, an argument which is well documented by Adams (1995). In the context of criminology, awareness of these general processes (potentially) returns us to the question of the state in both hiding the crimes which are defined as risky and those which are not as well as hiding the implication of the state in such processes.

This discussion so far has addressed some of the general problems inherent in an uncritical acceptance of a conventional understanding of risk and risk analysis. A more specific analysis, which carries with it quite focused implications for the criminological exploration of risk is raised in the following extract from Douglas:

> In spite of evidence to the contrary, avoiding loss is written into the psychology textbooks as the normal, rational, human motive. But all this means is that the commercial, risk-averse culture has locally vanquished the risk-seeking culture, and writes off the latter as pathological or abnormal. To ignore such a large segment of the human psychology tells us more about the assumptions upholding the modern industrial way of life than about human nature's risk-taking propensities.
>
> (Douglas, 1992: 30)

In one sense, it could be argued that both criminology and victimology have implicitly accepted this modern version of the risk averse culture which Douglas talks about. This emphasis on risk avoidance is deeply embedded in the discourses around crime prevention which emanate from theories of all political hues. It also reflects a version of (masculine) knowledge which prefers to assert control via reasonable and rational argument rather than by brute force through the management of risk (risk assessment).

In other words, what is to be found in the criminological and victimological literature is a version of knowledge which values reason, in which risk avoidance is presumed to be reasonable and risk seeking behaviour is presumed to be unreasonable. As a consequence risk seeking behaviour is downgraded, obscured, hidden from the debate though not necessarily from social reality or individual experience. That these values concur with those which support a conventional view of science and what counts as scientific knowledge is, therefore, of no great surprise.

It is the pervasiveness of this search for 'zero risk' which facilitates an understanding of the way in which the criminological and victimological agendas have been set, especially in relation to crime prevention. The search for the cause of crime has never been that separate from the search for the control of crime – crime prevention. An emphasis on risk avoidance fits so much more neatly in a discipline implicated in the policy making process in this way. However, the effects of adopting an implicit zero risk position are far reaching. This is especially the case in relation to constructing an adequate understanding of both the cause and the effect of criminal behaviour and the nature and extent of criminal victimization.

To summarize: criminology's (and victimology's) implicit acceptance of a conventional scientific agenda and its associated modernist and masculinist stance has resulted in that discipline's failure to work more critically with the concept of risk. This failure, as Chapter 7 implied, has impoverished criminology's understanding of the experience of criminal victimization by tying that issue, and by implication any associated explanation of criminal behaviour, to a presumption of risk avoidance, that is a 'rational' view of the risk management of behaviour. Hence what is deemed to be an appropriate policy stance with respect to repeat victimization.

In addition this failure has resulted in, for the most part, a masculinist interpretation of, and debate around, what counts as risky behaviour, endorsing some behaviours for men as acceptably risking and some behaviours for women as unacceptably risky. Both sides of this coin downgrading the potential value of exploring the pleasures of crime (as alluded to in Chapter 5) and emphasizing the apparent victimhood of women (also alluded to in Chapter 5). For example, in the context of the 'fear of crime' debate, this failure has impacted upon the way in which much criminological work hides men's fears (and their thrills) and simultaneously consigns women to possessing 'legitimate fears'.

To summarize: the criminological and victimological analysis of risk reflects the extent to which both these areas of study are tied implicitly to particular conceptions of the knowledge production process and the role of the scientific endeavour in that process. In particular the failure to explore risk as both a gendered concept as well as a gendered experience has limited both of these disciplinary agendas in different but pervasive ways.

Attempts have been made to challenge these assumptions. Some of which have been referred to in Chapter 4 and some of which are related more directly to the fear of crime debate in which these issues appear have their most visible salience (see Sparks, 1992; Walklate, 1997). All of these efforts demonstrate that it is possible to work with alternative conceptualizations of risk that have the potential for enhancing criminological work. However, risk is only one side of a two sided relationship. The other side of this relationship is trust. It is to an exploration of that concept which we shall now turn.

Criminology and trust

As a general rule, trust arises when a community shares a set of moral values in such a way as to create expectations of regular honest behaviour.

(Fukuyama, 1996: 153)

The concept of trust has been relatively underexplored in the social sciences. In discussing the question of 'ontological security' Giddens (1991) has argued that trust is most clearly evidenced in traditional societies through kinship relations, local communities or religious commitment. However, the absence of these mechanisms in late modern societies renders trust no more than a matter for individual contractual negotiation. A similar argument is presented by Luhmann (1989). Gellner (1989) too argues that urban life is incompatible with trust and social cohesion suggesting that such processes are rooted in rural, tribal traditions. Yet as Fukuyama (1996) implies, trust is also an essential part of modern life. Without it economic relations cannot flourish, neither can they be completely controlled. Trust is therefore essential.

The kinds of trust which exist, however, may not always be necessarily about creating 'regular honest behaviour' as Fukuyama (1996) states. It may just as likely be about creating regular dishonest behaviour. It is the regularity or otherwise of behaviour which sustains or threatens social relationships. It is within this notion of regular social expectations that the question of trust becomes pertinent to criminology and victimology. This requires further exploration.

Arguably work emanating from the feminist movement, especially radical feminism, has been implicitly and explicitly concerned to problematize the question of trust in relation to women's experiences of criminal victimization. That work has clearly rendered problematic the notion of the safe haven of the home. Put another way, it has challenged the view that women need not fear men that they know: work colleagues, boyfriends, relatives. These were 'trustworthy' men. The view that 'All men are potential rapists' offers a definite challenge to such a presumption. The recognition that the familiar and the familial are not necessarily any more trustworthy than the stranger, puts a very different picture on the screen of who is and who is not trustworthy, a picture which feminist research has demonstrated routinely informs women's sense of 'ontological security'. Such work implies that just as the concept of risk is gendered so might be the concept of trust.

So in some respects a conceptualization of trust has been implicit in both mainstream and more radical versions of criminology and victimology. However, trust has never been a central concern in the social sciences in general let alone in the specialized area of crime (Misztal, 1996). Yet it is clear that as social life becomes increasingly more complex and some would say increasingly more confused and confusing, the question of trust is becoming more visible. This greater visibility raises both theoretical and empirical questions.

Giddens (1991) and Beck (1992) both argue that the increasing awareness of the importance of trust is the concomitant effect of greater awareness of the possible future damage of risk taking activity alongside the challenge to universalism posed by postmodernism. As Misztal states:

> By destroying the grounds for believing in a universal truth, post-modernity does not make our lives more easy but only less constrained by rules and more contingent. It demands new solutions based on the tolerant co-existence of a diversity of cultures. Yet although post modernism encourages us to live without an enemy, it stops short of offering constructive bases for mutual understanding and trust.
>
> (Misztal, 1996: 239)

In a sense this quote endorses the view of Fukuyama (1996) expressed earlier. It certainly centres the need for understanding the changing nature of trust especially in the context of social relationships which are increasingly characterized by diversity and the celebration of difference. In order to 'live without an enemy' requires trust. But how does trust manifest itself? The relevance of this question has been explored in the criminological context by Nelken (1994).

The value of exploring the question of trust is raised by Nelken (1994) in the context of the importance to criminology of engaging in comparative research. This is an issue we shall return to, however part of Nelken's argument is that out of comparative research it is possible to further criminology *theoretically*. In his review of what might be learned by engaging in a comparative analysis of white collar and/or corporate crime, Nelken (1994) suggests that a number of questions become pertinent for criminology. These questions are as follows. Whom can you trust? How do you trust? How much can you trust? When can you trust?

Given the nature of international crime patterns in general and corporate criminal activities in particular, it is possible to see the validity of Nelken's argument in this respect. It is an argument which certainly resonates with the analysis of more and less successful economies offered by Fukuyama (1996) in which he also centres the question of trust. Moreover, these are a range of questions which are more or less implicit to feminist work on sexual violence as suggested above. The value of these questions for criminology, however, transcends these concerns. This statement requires justification.

Anderson and Davey (1995) have reported on the increasing influence of the ideas of 'communitarianism'. Led by the American social scientist Etzioni, this school of thought believes that 'we need to create "a new moral, social, and public order based on restored communities, without allowing puritanism or oppression" '(Anderson and Davey, 1995: 18). The importance of invoking the concept of the community as a vehicle for generating and managing social change has been espoused by those on both the left and the right of the political spectrum. This is nowhere more the case than in the arena of crime and crime prevention. Here community crime prevention initiatives have proliferated since the early 1980s. A central dilemma posed by these policy responses is, however, what is meant by community and how is an understanding of community to be constructed, if at all, by those subjected to these policy responses? It is in this latter respect that the importance of understanding how trust operates re-emerges.

The mechanisms and processes identified by Evans, Fraser and Walklate (1996) in one high crime community testify to the importance of understanding the nature of trust, they argue that:

> your *place* in relation to crime *places* you in a community of belonging and exclusion . . . It is consequently important to recognise who is seen to be protecting you and how: for many people it is not the police or the council but local families and/or the Salford Firm. Moreover it is the absence of confidence in the formal agencies which creates the space for those other forces to come into play.
>
> (Evans *et al.*, 1996: 379)

For people living in the locality being referred to above, the question of trusting other local people because they were local and not trusting the police or other formal agencies was quite a complex process, but nevertheless their sense of 'ontological security' (Giddens, 1991) was certainly informed by these processes. Thus raising a range of tensions between the professionals' image of this community and what would or would not work in the area and those views of the people living in the area. For local people the area was perceived to be safe despite its high crime profile.

Such tensions return us to the issue raised earlier concerning whose knowledge counts as legitimate and under what circumstances. They also highlight the importance of understanding the nature of the diversity surrounding the crime question and the impact that may have on the policy process. They certainly manifest the importance of understanding the tensions around different constructions of risk and trust and how they are articulated. Arguably, however, this discussion returns us to the third issue relevant to a further development of the criminological and victimological agendas: the relationship between the citizen and the state.

Criminology, the citizen and the state

The work reported by Evans *et al.* (1996) was rooted in a locality from which for the most part the state had withdrawn. Perceived from the outside as an area in which the underclass was to be found it bore all the hallmarks of the 'dangerous classes' discussed in Chapter 6. There are other similar locations throughout the UK (Campbell, 1993). These are the locations which have suffered disproportionately as the gap between rich and poor has grown since the mid-1980s and the changing relationship between the citizen and the state (also discussed in Chapter 6) has become more deeply embedded. Arguably, then, how people manage their routine daily lives informed by the concepts of risk and trust constitute the surface manifestation of this deeper structural relationship: the relationship between the citizen and the state.

Understanding the nature of this structural relationship reveals much about the mechanisms of social inclusion and exclusion and how those mechanisms work. Placing this relationship at the centre of criminological concern does not presume that the state, the institutions of the state, or any individual, necessarily operates in a conspiratorial manner. However, it does presume that the risks we are encouraged to see as opposed to those which we are not serve the interests of the state. Hence the undoubted value of comparative research of both a theoretical and an empirical nature in order to better explore and expose such processes. Neither does this view necessarily imply that individual citizens are cultural dopes; but it does assert that to understand how they are constructed in terms of legitimacy, does frame the options present in their everyday lives. The substantial validity of this viewpoint has been asserted in Chapters 6 and 7.

Conclusion

In summing up, then, a number of themes suggest themselves. It is clear that criminology has much yet to learn from both feminism and postmodernism in their endeavours to problematize both the nature of knowledge and the knowledge construction process and how this may or may not relate to the policy arena. Both of these areas of debate render problematic the notion of 'Crime' and 'Policy'. The questions raised by these areas of concern, however, do not necessarily lead to a retreat into relativism but may demand a more careful working with what is known, how, where and when and what might work under what circumstances. It is clear that centring a more refined understanding of the concepts of risk and trust and the underlying relationship that these concepts rest upon, might lead to far more fruitful theoretical and empirical agendas for both criminology and victimology. This would certainly be the case if such agendas were set in a comparative context, and especially if that context were a European one.

Glossary

Categorical theory   A concern with the ways in which the social construction of the terms 'man' and 'woman' impact upon the lives of individuals.

Citizenship   A term encompassing those who are included and excluded from the rewards of the social system.

Crime   Lawbreaking behaviour.

Left realism   A way of thinking about crime largely emanating from the United Kingdom in the mid-1980s, concerned to take crime seriously and to reclaim the law and order debate from right wing politics.

Liberal feminism   A concern to redress the sex balance by ensuring women are included in the intellectual and empirical process.

Modern   Taken to characterize societies in which the power of reason has superseded the power of belief.

Multiple and/or repeat victimization   Concern with patterns of victimization resulting in a small proportion of the total number of victims experiencing most of the victimization.

Positivism   One way of thinking about knowledge and the knowledge production process which centres that which can be objectively observed and/or measured.

Positivist criminology   A process of gathering the facts concerning the causes of crime.

Positivist victimology   A process of gathering the facts concerning the causes of victimization.

Postmodern feminism   That feminist work which celebrates the differences between women and challenges any claim to universal knowledge.

Radical feminism   Work which is concerned to address men's oppression of women.

Right realism   Largely emanating from the United States, this label refers to a collection of theoretical and policy concerns about crime which centre the cause of crime within the individual.

Sex role theory   Takes as given the biological origins of the differences between men and women.

Social justice   The way in which any society organizes itself to distribute the rewards and punishments in that society.

Socialist feminism   Feminist work appreciating the ways in which age, sex, gender and class weave a complex web on women's lives.

Underclass   A term often used in the 1990s to refer to those sections of society who live outside its mechanisms of rewards.

References

Adams, J. (1995) *Risk*. London: UCL Press.

Anderson, P. and Davey, K. (1995) Import duties. *New Statesman and Society*, 3 March: 18–23.

Barbelet, J. M. (1988) *Citizenship*. Milton Keynes: Open University Press.

Beck, U. (1992) *The Risk Society*. London: Sage.

Becker, H. (1963) *The Outsiders*. New York: Free Press.

Bell, D. (1976) *The Cultural Contradictions of Capitalism*. London: Heinemann.

Bernstein, P. L. (1996) *Against the Gods: The Remarkable Story of Risk*. New York: Wiley.

Bhaskar, R. (1978) *A Realist Theory of Science*. Brighton: Harvester.

Booth, C. (ed.) (1892–1903) *Life and Labour of the People in London*, 7 vols. London: Macmillan.

Bottoms, A. E. (1983) Neglected features of the contemporary penal system, in D. Garland and P. Young (eds) *The Power to Punish*. London: Heinemann.

Bowlby, J. (1965) *Child Care and the Growth of Love*. Harmondsworth: Penguin.

Box, S. (1987) *Recession, Crime and Punishment*. London: Macmillan.

Braithwaite, J. (1989) *Crime, Shame and Reintegration*. Cambridge: Cambridge University Press.

Brake, M. and Hale, C. (1992) *Public Order and Private Lives*. London: Routledge.

Brittain, A. (1989) *Masculinity and Power*. Oxford: Basil Blackwell.

Brogden, M., Jefferson, T. and Walklate, S. (1988) *Introducing Policework*. London: Unwin Hyman.

Brown, B. (1986) Women and crime: the dark figures of criminology. *Economy and Society* 15(3): 33–56.

Brown, D. and Hogg, R. (1992) Law and order politics – left realism and radical criminology: a view from down under, in R. Matthews and J. Young (eds) *Issues in Realist Criminology*. London: Sage.

Brown, J. C. (1990) The focus on single mothers, in C. Murray (ed.) *The Emerging British Underclass*. London: Institute of Economic Affairs.

Cain, M. (1986) Realism, feminism, methodology and law. *International Journal of Sociology of Law* 14: 255–67.

Cain, M. (1990a) Realist philosophy and standpoint epistemologies or feminist criminology as a successor science, in L. Gelsthorpe and A. Morris (eds) *Feminist Perspectives in Criminology*. Milton Keynes: Open University Press.

Cain, M. (1990b) Towards transgression: new directions in feminist criminology. *International Journal of the Sociology of Law* 18: 1–18.

Cameron, D. and Fraser, E. (1987) *The Lust to Kill*. Oxford: Polity Press.

Campbell, B. (1993) *Goliath: Britain's Dangerous Places*. London: Virago.

Carlen, P. (1983) *Women's Imprisonment*. London: Routledge and Kegan Paul.

Carlen, P. (1988) *Women, Crime and Poverty*. Milton Keynes: Open University Press.

Carlen, P. (1990) Women, crime, feminism and realism. *Social Justice* 17(4): 106–23.

Carlen, P. (1992) Criminal women and criminal justice: the limits to and potential of feminist and left realist perspectives, in R. Matthews and J. Young (eds) *Issues in Realist Criminology*. London: Sage.

Carlen, P. (1996) *Jigsaw: A Political Criminology of Youth Homelessness*. Buckingham: Open University Press.

Chambers, G. and Millar, A. (1983) *Investigating Sexual Assault*. Edinburgh: Scottish Office.

Chambliss, W. J. (1975) Towards a political economy of crime. *Theory and Society* 2: 149–70.

Clarke, R. (1980) Situational crime prevention: theory and practice. *British Journal of Criminology* 20(2): 136–47.

Cloward, R. and Ohlin, L. (1960) *Delinquency and Opportunity: A Theory of Delinquent Gangs*. New York: Free Press.

Cohen, A. K. (1955) *Delinquent Boys*. London: Free Press.

Cohen, L. E. and Felson, M. (1979) Social change and crime rate trends: a routine activity approach. *American Sociological Review* 44(4): 588–608.

Coleman, C. and Moynihan, J. (1996) *Understanding Crime Data*. Buckingham: Open University Press.

Connell, R. W. (1987) *Gender and Power*. Oxford: Polity Press.

Cook, D. (1989) *Rich Law, Poor Law*. Milton Keynes: Open University Press.

Cooke, P. (1990) *Back to the Future*. London: Unwin Hyman.

Cornish, D. and Clarke, R. V. (1986) *The Reasoning Criminal: Rational Choice Perspectives on Offending*. New York: Springer.

Cowie, J., Cowie, V. and Slater, E. (1968) *Delinquency and Girls*. London: Heinemann.

Crawford, A., Jones, T., Woodhouse, T. and Young, J. (1990) *The Second Islington Crime Survey*. Barnet: Centre for Criminology, Middlesex Polytechnic.

Criminal Statistics for England and Wales (1993) London: HMSO.

Currie, E. (1985) *Confronting Crime*. New York: Pantheon.

Currie, E. (1995) The end of work: public and private livelihood in post-employment capitalism, in S. Edgell, S. Walklate and G. Williams (eds) *Debating the Future of the Public Sphere*. Aldershot: Avebury.

Dahrendorf, R. (1992) Footnotes to the discussion, in D. J. Smith (ed.) *Understanding the Underclass*. London: Policy Studies Institute.

Datesmann, S. and Scarpitti, F. (eds) (1980) *Women, Crime and Justice*. New York: Oxford University Press.

DeFleur, L. B. (1975) Biasing influences and drug arrest records. *American Sociological Review* 40: 88–103.

Dekeseredy, W. and Schwartz, M. (1991) British left realism on the abuse of women: a critical appraisal, in H. Pepinsky and R. Quinney (eds) *Criminology as Peacemaking*. Bloomington, IN: Indiana University Press.

Dennis, N. (1993) *Rising Crime and the Dismembered Family*. London: Institute of Economic Affairs.

Dennis, N. and Erdos, G. (1992) *Families without Fatherhood*. London: Institute of Economic Affairs.

Dobash, R. P., Dobash, R. E. and Gutteridge, S. (1986) *The Imprisonment of Women*. Oxford: Basil Blackwell.

Douglas, M. (1992) *Risk and Blame: Essays in Cultural Theory*. London: Routledge.

Downes, D. M. and Rock, P. (1988) *Understanding Deviance*. Oxford: Oxford University Press.

Eagle-Russett, C. (1989) *Sexual Science: The Victorian Construction of Motherhood*. Cambridge, MA: Harvard University Press.

Eaton, M. (1986) *Justice for Women?* Milton Keynes: Open University Press.

Edgar, D. (1991) Are you being served? *Marxism Today*, May.

Edwards, S. (1989) *Policing 'Domestic' Violence*. London: Sage.

Elias, R. (1985) Transcending our social reality of victimization: towards a new victimology of human rights. *Victimology* 10: 6–25.

Elias, R. (1986) *The Politics of Victimization*. Oxford: Oxford University Press.

Elias, R. (1993) *Victims Still: The Political Manipulation of Crime Victims*. London: Sage.

Evans, K., Fraser, P. and Walklate, S. (1996) Whom can you trust? The politics of grassing on an inner city housing estate. *Sociological Review* 44(3): 361–80.

Eysenck, H. and Gudjonnson, G. H. (1990) *The Causes and Cures of Crime*. New York: Plenum.

Farrell, G. (1992) Multiple victimisation: its extent and significance. *International Review of Victimology* 2(2):85–102.

Farrington, D. P. and Morris, A. M. (1983) Sex, sentencing and reconviction. *British Journal of Criminology* 23(3):229–48.

Fattah, E. (1991) *Understanding Criminal Victimization*. Scarborough, Ontario: Prentice-Hall.

Fattah, E. A. (ed.) (1992) *Critical Victimology*. London: Macmillan.

Felson, M. (1994) *Crime and Everyday Life*. Thousand Oaks, CA: Pine Forge Press.

Field, F. (1990) Britain's underclass: countering the growth, in C. Murray (ed.) *The Emerging British Underclass*. London: Institute of Economic Affairs.

Foucault, M. (1977) *Discipline and Punish*. Harmondsworth: Penguin.

Fukuyama, F. (1996) *Trust*. Harmondsworth: Penguin.

Galtung, J. (1967) *Theory and Method of Social Research*. London: Allen and Unwin.

Garland, D. (1985) *Punishment and Welfare*. Aldershot: Gower.

Garland, D. (1988) British criminology before 1935. *British Journal of Criminology* 28(2): 1–17.

Garland, D. (1994) Of crimes and criminals: the development of criminology in Britain, in M. Maguire, R. Morgan and R. Reiner (eds) *The Oxford Handbook of Criminology*. Oxford: Oxford University Press

Garofalo, J. (1986) Lifestyle and victimization: an update, in E. A. Fattah (ed.) *From Crime Policy to Victim Policy*. London: Macmillan.

Gellner, E. (1989) Trust, cohesion and the social order, in D. Gambetta (ed.) *Trust: Making and Breaking Co-operative Relations*. London: Basil Blackwell.

Gelsthorpe, L. (1989) *Sexism and the Female Offender*. Aldershot: Gower.

Gelsthorpe, L. and Morris, A. (eds) (1990) *Feminist Perspectives in Criminology.* Buckingham: Open University Press.

Genn, H. (1988) Multiple victimization, in M. Maguire and J. Pointing (eds) *Victims of Crime: A New Deal?* Milton Keynes: Open University Press.

George, V. and Wilding, P. (1976) *Ideology and Social Welfare.* London: Routledge and Kegan Paul.

Gibbons, D. C. (1994) *Talking about Crime and Criminals.* Englewood Cliffs, NJ: Prentice-Hall.

Giddens, A. (1984) *The Constitution of Society.* Cambridge: Polity Press.

Giddens, A. (1991) *Modernity and Self Identity.* Oxford: Basil Blackwell.

Gimenez, M. (1990) The feminization of poverty. *Social Justice* 17(3): 43–69.

Glueck, S. and Glueck, E. (1950) *Unravelling Juvenile Delinquency.* Cambridge, MA: Harvard University Press.

Goring, C. (1913) *The English Convict.* London: HMSO.

Harding, S. (1991) *Whose Science? Whose Knowledge?* Milton Keynes: Open University Press.

Heath, A. (1992) The attitudes of the underclass, in D. J. Smith (ed.) *Understanding the Underclass.* London: Policy Studies Institute.

Heidensohn, F. (1985) *Women and Crime.* London: Macmillan.

Hentig, H. von (1948) *The Criminal and his Victim.* New Haven, CT: Yale University Press.

Hindelang, M. J. (1979) Sex differences in criminal activity. *Social Problems,* 27: 143–56.

Hindelang, M. J., Gottfredson, M. R. and Garofalo, J. (1978) *Victims of Personal Crime: An Empirical Foundation for a Theory of Personal Victimization.* Cambridge, MA: Ballinger.

Hope, T. and Walklate, S. (1995) Repeat victimisation: differentiation or structuration? Paper presented to the British Criminology Conference, Loughborough, July.

Hough, M. and Mayhew, P. (1983) *The 1982 British Crime Survey.* London: HMSO.

Hurd, D. (1989) *Independent,* 14 September.

Hutton, W. (1994) A question of relativity, *Search,* 20 (summer).

Hutton, W. (1995) *The State We're In.* London: Random House.

Jefferson, T. (1993) Theorising masculine subjectivity. Plenary address, Masculinities and Crime Conference, Brunel University, September.

Jefferson, T., Sim, J. and Walklate, S. (1992) Europe, the left and criminology in the 1990s: accountability, control and the social construction of the consumer, in D. Farrington and S. Walklate (eds) *Offenders and Victims: Theory and Policy.* London: British Society of Criminology and Institute for the Study and Treatment of Delinquency.

Jonkers, J. (1986) *Victims of Violence.* London: Fontana.

Karmen, A. (1990) *Crime Victims: An Introduction to Victimology.* Pacific Grove, CA: Brooks Cole.

Katz, J. (1988) *The Seductions of Crime.* New York: Basic Books.

Kinsey, R., Lea, J. and Young, J. (1986) *Losing the Fight Against Crime.* Oxford: Basil Blackwell.

Kretschmer, E. (1926) *Physique and Character.* New York: Harcourt Brace Jovanovich.

Leonard, E. B. (1982) *A Critique of Criminology Theory: Women, Crime and Society.* London: Longman.

Lewis, J. (1980) *The Politics of Motherhood*. London: Croom Helm.

Lilly, J. R., Cullen, F. and Ball, R. (1995) *Criminological Theory: Context and Consequences*. Thousand Oaks, CA: Sage.

Lister, R. (1990) *The Exclusive Society: Citizenship and the Poor*. London: Child Poverty Action Group.

Lowman, J. (1992) Rediscovering crime, in J. Young and R. Matthews (eds) *Rethinking Criminology: The Realist Debate*. London: Sage.

Lowman, J. and MacLean, B. (eds) (1992) *Realist Criminology: Crime Control and Policing in the 1990s*. Toronto: University of Toronto Press.

Luhmann, N. (1989) Familiarity, confidence, trust: problems and alternatives, in D. Gambetta (ed.) *Trust: Making and Breaking Co-operative Relations*. London: Basil Blackwell.

MacIntyre, A. (1988) *Whose Justice? Which Rationality?* London: Duckworth.

MacKinnon, C. (1989) *Towards a Feminist Theory of the State*. Cambridge, MA: Harvard University Press.

MacLean, B. (1992) A programme of local crime survey research for Canada, in J. Lowman and B. MacLean (eds) *Realist Criminology: Crime Control and Policing in the 1990s*. Toronto: University of Toronto Press.

Maguire, M. and Pointing, J. (1988) *Victims of Crime: A New Deal?* Milton Keynes: Open University Press.

Marshall, T. H. (1981[1948]) *The Rights to Welfare and Other Essays*. London: Heinemann.

Matthews, N. (1994) *Confronting Rape*. London: Routledge.

Matthews, R. and Young, J. (eds) (1992) *Issues in Realist Criminology*. London: Sage.

Mawby, R. and Walklate, S. (1994) *Critical Victimology: The Victim in International Perspective*. London: Sage.

Mayhew, P. and Hough, M. (1988) The British Crime Survey: origins and impact, in M. Maguire and J. Pointing (eds) *Victims of Crime: A New Deal?* Milton Keynes: Open University Press.

Mendelsohn, B. (1974) The origins of the doctrine of victimology, in I. Drapkin and E. Vicano (eds) *Victimology*. Lexington, IN: D.C. Heath and Co.

Merton, R. K. (1938) Social structure and anomie. *American Sociological Review* 3: 672–82.

Merton, R. K. (1968) *Social Theory and Social Structure*. New York: Free Press.

Messerschmidt, J. (1986) *Capitalism, Patriarchy and Crime: Towards a Socialist Feminist Criminology*. Totowa, NJ: Rowman and Littlefield.

Messerschmidt, J. (1993) *Masculinities and Crime*. Lanham, MD: Rowman and Littlefield.

Miers, D. (1978) *Responses to Victimization*. Abingdon: Professional Books.

Miers, D. (1989) Positivist victimology: a critique. *International Review of Victimology* 1(1): 3–22.

Miers, D. (1990) Positivist victimology: a critique part 2. *International Review of Victimology* 1(3): 219–30.

Misztal, B. (1996) *Trust in Modern Societies*. Oxford: Polity Press.

Mooney, J. (1993) The North London Domestic Violence Survey. Paper presented to British Criminology Conference, Cardiff, July.

Morris, A. (1987) *Women, Crime and Criminal Justice*. Oxford: Basil Blackwell.

Morris, L. (1994) *Dangerous Classes: The Underclass and Social Citizenship.* London: Routledge.

Morris, T. (1989) *Crime and Criminal Justice since 1945.* Oxford: Basil Blackwell.

Mouffe, C. (1988) The civics lesson, *New Statesman and Society* 7 October: 28–31.

Mugford, G. and O'Malley, P. (1990) Heroin policy and deficit models. The limits of left realism, unpublished paper.

Muncie, J., McLaughlin, E. and Langan, M. (eds) (1996) *Criminological Perspectives: A Reader.* London: Sage.

Murray, C. (1990) *The Emerging British Underclass.* London: Institute of Economic Affairs.

Naffine, N. (1987) *Female Crime.* Sydney: Allen and Unwin.

Naffine, N. (1990) *Law and the Sexes.* London: Allen and Unwin.

Nelken, D. (1994) Whom can you trust? The future of comparative criminology, in D. Nelken (ed.) *The Future of Criminology.* London: Sage.

Offe, C. (1984) *Contradictions of the Welfare State.* London: Heinemann.

Offe, C. and Ronge, V. (1975) Theses on the theory of the state. *New German Critique* 6 (Fall): 139–47.

Outhwaite, W. (1987) *New Philosophies of Social Science: Realism, Hermeneutics and Critical Theory.* London: Macmillan.

Painter, K. (1991) *Marriage, Wife Rape and the Law.* Manchester: Department of Social Policy, University of Manchester.

Parsons, T. (1937) *The Structure of Social Action.* New York: McGraw-Hill.

Phipps, A. (1988) Ideologies, political parties, and victims of crime, in M. Maguire and J. Pointing (eds) *Victims of Crime: A New Deal?* Milton Keynes: Open University Press.

Pollak, O. (1950) *The Criminality of Women.* New York: A. S. Barnes/Perpetua.

Quinney, R. (1972) Who is the victim? *Criminology* November: 309–29.

Quinney, R. (1977) *Class, State and Crime: On the Theory and Practice of Criminal Justice.* New York: McKay.

Reiner, R. (1985) *The Politics of the Police.* Hemel Hempstead: Harvester Wheatsheaf.

Rock, P. (1986) *A View from the Shadows.* Oxford: Clarendon.

Rock, P. (1990) *Helping Victims of Crime: The Home Office and the Rise of Victim Support in England and Wales.* Oxford: Clarendon.

Rock, P. (ed.) (1994) *History of Criminology.* Aldershot: Darmouth.

Roshier, B. (1989) *Controlling Crime.* Milton Keynes: Open University Press.

Runciman, W. G. (1990) How many classes are there in contemporary British society? *Sociology* 24(3): 377–96.

Russell, D. (1990) *Rape in Marriage.* New York: Collier.

Scott, J. (1994) *Wealth and Poverty.* London: Macmillan.

Scraton, P. (1990) Scientific knowledge or masculine discourses? Challenging patriarchy in criminology, in L. Gelsthorpe and A. Morris (eds) *Feminist Perspectives in Criminology.* Buckingham: Open University Press.

Scraton, P. and Chadwick, K. (1991) The theoretical and political priorities of critical criminology, in K. Stenson and D. Cowell (eds) *The Politics of Crime Control.* London: Sage.

Scully, D. (1990) *Understanding Sexual Violence.* London: Unwin Hyman.

Seidler, V. (1994) *Unreasonable Men: Masculinity and Social Theory*. London: Routledge.

Short, J. (1984) The social fabric at risk: toward the social transformation of risk analysis. *American Sociological Review* 49 (December): 711–25.

Sim, J., Scraton, P. and Gordon, P. (1987) Introduction: crime, the state, and critical analysis, in P. Scraton (ed.) *Law, Order and the Authoritarian State*. Milton Keynes: Open University Press.

Smart, C. (1977) *Women, Crime and Criminology*. London: Routledge and Kegan Paul.

Smart, C. (1989) *Feminism and the Power of Law*. London: Routledge.

Smart, C. (1990) Feminist approaches to criminology: or postmodern woman meets atavistic man, in L. Gelsthorpe and A. Morris (eds) *Feminist Perspectives in Criminology*. Milton Keynes: Open University Press.

Smith, D. J. (1992) Defining the underclass, in D. J. Smith (ed.) *Understanding the Underclass*. London: Policy Studies Institute.

Sparks, R. (1992) Reason and unreason in left realism: some problems in the constitution of the fear of crime, in R. Matthews and J. Young (eds) *Issues in Realist Criminology*. London: Sage.

Sparks, R., Genn, H. and Dodd, D. (1977) *Surveying Victims*. Chichester: Wiley.

Stanko, E. A. (1985) *Intimate Intrusions: Women's Experience of Male Violence*. London: Virago.

Stanley, L. and Wise, S. (1987) *Georgie, Porgie: Sexual Harassment in Everyday Life*. London: Pandora.

Stenson, K. and Brearly, N. (1989) Left realism in criminology and the return to consensus theory, in R. Reiner and M. Cross (eds) *Beyond Law and Order*. London: Macmillan.

Stone, L. (1995) *Uncertain Unions and Broken Lives*. Oxford: Oxford University Press.

Sumner, C. (1990) *Censure, Politics and Criminal Justice*. Milton Keynes: Open University Press.

Sutherland, E. H. (1947) *Principles of Criminology*. Philadelphia, PA: Lippincott.

Taylor, I., Walton, P. and Young, J. (1973) *The New Criminology*. London: Routledge and Kegan Paul.

Thatcher, M. (1977) *Let our Children Grow Tall*. London: Centre for Policy Studies.

Tolson, A. (1977) *The Limits of Masculinity*. London: Tavistock.

Tuck, M. (1993) Research and public policy, in A. Coote (ed.) *Families, Children and Crime*. London: Institute for Public Policy Research.

The United States President's Task Force on Victims of Crime (1982) *Final Report*. Washington, DC: US Government Printing Office.

Utting, D. (1993) Family factors and the rise of crime, in A. Coote (ed.) *Families, Children and Crime*. London: Institute for Public Policy Research.

Walklate, S. (1989) *Victimology: The Victim and the Criminal Justice Process*. London: Unwin Hyman.

Walklate, S. (1990) Researching victims of crime: critical victimology. *Social Justice* 17(3): 25–42.

Walklate, S. (1992) Responding to domestic violence: an evaluation of the work of the 'dedicated' unit in D division. Final report to Merseyside Police. Salford: Department of Sociology: University of Salford.

Walklate, S. (1995) *Gender and Crime*. Hemel Hempstead: Harvester Wheatsheaf.

Walklate, S. (1996) Can there be a feminist victimology?, in P. Davies, P. Francis and V. Jupp (eds) *Understanding Victimization: Themes and Perspectives*. Newcastle: University of Northumbria Press.

Walklate, S. (1997) Risk and criminal victimization: a modernist dilemma? *British Journal of Criminology* 37(1): 35–45.

Wildavsky, A. (1988) *Searching for Safety*. Oxford: Transition.

Williams, F. P. and McShane, M. D. (1994) *Criminological Theory*. New Jersey: Prentice Hall.

Wilson, E. (1983) *What Is to be Done about Violence Against Women?* Harmondsworth: Penguin.

Wilson, J. Q. (1975) *Thinking about Crime*. New York: Vintage.

Wilson, J. Q. and Herrnstein, R. (1985) *Crime and Human Nature*. New York: Simon and Schuster.

Wootton, B. (1959) *Social Science and Social Pathology*. London: Allen and Unwin.

Young, A. (1992) Feminism and the body of criminology, in D. P. Farrington and S. Walklate (eds) *Offenders and Victims: Theory and Policy*. London: British Society of Criminology and Institute for the Study and Treatment of Delinquency.

Young, A. (1996) *Imagining Crime*. London: Sage.

Young, J. (1986) The failure of criminology: the need for a radical realism, in R. Matthews and J. Young (eds) *Confronting Crime*. London: Sage.

Young, J. (1988) Risk of crime and the fear of crime: a realist critique of survey based assumptions, in M. Maguire and J. Pointing (eds) *Victims of Crime: A New Deal?* Milton Keynes: Open University Press.

Young, J. (1992) Ten points of realism, in J. Young and R. Matthews (eds) *Rethinking Criminology: The Realist Debate*. London: Sage.

Young, J. (1994) Incessant chatter: recent paradigms in criminology, in M. Maguire, R. Morgan and R. Reiner (eds) *The Oxford Handbook of Criminology*. Oxford: Oxford University Press.

Young, J. and Matthews, R. (eds) (1992) *Rethinking Criminology: The Realist Debate*. London: Sage.

Zedner, L. (1994) Victims, in M. Maguire, R. Morgan and R. Reiner (eds) *The Oxford Handbook of Criminology*. Oxford: Oxford University Press.

Index

UNDERSTANDING JUSTICE
AN INTRODUCTION TO IDEAS, PERSPECTIVES AND CONTROVERSIES IN MODERN PENAL THEORY

Barbara A. Hudson

- Why should offenders be punished – what should punishments be designed to achieve?
- Why has imprisonment become the *normal* punishment for crime in modern industrial societies?
- What is the relationship between theories of punishment and the actual penalties inflicted on offenders?

Understanding justice is one of a series of student textbooks designed to cover the major areas of debate within the fields of criminology, criminal justice and penology. It provides a comprehensive account of the ideas and controversies that have arisen within law, philosophy, sociology and criminology about the punishment of criminals. Written in a clear, accessible style, it summarizes major philosophical ideas – retribution, rehabilitation, incapacitation – and discusses their strengths and weaknesses.

The sociological perspectives of Durkheim, the Marxists, Foucault and their contemporary followers are analysed and assessed. A section on the criminological perspective on punishment looks at the influence of theory on penal policy, and at the impact of penal ideologies on those on whom punishment is inflicted. The contributions of feminist theorists, and the challenges they pose to masculinist accounts of punishment, are included. The concluding chapter presents critiques of the very idea of punishment, and looks at contemporary proposals which could make society's response to crime less dependent on punishment than at present.

Understanding justice has been designed for students from a range of disciplines and is suitable for a variety of crime-related courses in sociology, social policy, law and social work. It will also be useful to professionals in criminal justice agencies and to all those interested in understanding the issues behind public and political debates on punishment.

Contents
Perspectives on punishment – Part 1: The goals of punishment: the judicial perspective – Utilitarian approaches – Retribution – Hybrids, compromises and syntheses – Part 2: Punishment and modernity: the sociological perspective – Punishment and progress: the Durkheimian tradition – The political economy of punishment: Marxist approaches – The disciplined society: Foucault and the analysis of penality – Part 3: Towards justice? The struggle for justice: critical criminology and critical legal studies – Postscript: Beyond the modernity: the fate of justice – Glossary of key terms – Suggestions for further reading – References – Index.

192pp   0 335 19329 3 (Paperback)   0 335 19684 5 (Hardback)

UNDERSTANDING CRIME DATA
HAUNTED BY THE DARK FIGURE

Clive Coleman and Jenny Moynihan

- What are the main ways of acquiring numerical information about crime and offenders?
- How can we understand this information and avoid the various pitfalls of interpretation?
- What does the evidence tell us about the relationships between offending and age, sex, race, class, unemployment, and trends in crime over the years?

This clear and practical text breathes life into an essential subject that students have at times found uninspiring. It provides a guide to crime data for those with little background in the subject and at the same time, it will provide a source of reference for more experienced researchers. The authors have, for example, minimized as far as possible the presentation of detailed figures and complicated tables, but they have not avoided some of the more difficult issues that arise in interpreting and using such data.

Understanding crime data begins by locating the study and use of crime data within the theoretical and historical development of criminology, a subject that has long been haunted by the dark figure of hidden crime and offenders. Readers are guided through the development, limitations and uses of the three main sources of numerical crime data, and selected key issues in the interpretation of crime data are examined.

The characteristics of offenders are discussed with reference to the key variables of age, sex, race and class, and the difficulties involved in interpreting long- and short-term trends in the crime rate are highlighted. The authors assess what crime data can tell us about the relationships between crime and unemployment, and they conclude the book with their personal evaluation and prognosis of the field.

Understanding crime data is a well structured text for students of criminology, and it includes annotated further reading, lists of basic concepts, and a glossary for ease of reference. It will also have considerable appeal to professionals in criminal justice, probation and social work.

Contents
Haunted by the dark figure: criminologists as ghostbusters? – Official statistics: the authorized version? – Self-report studies: true confessions? – Victimization surveys: total recall? – Characteristics of offenders: the usual suspects? – Interpreting trends: quantum leaps? – Conclusion: carry on counting? – Glossary – References – Index

192pp   0 335 19518 0 (Paperback)   0 335 19519 9 (Hardback)